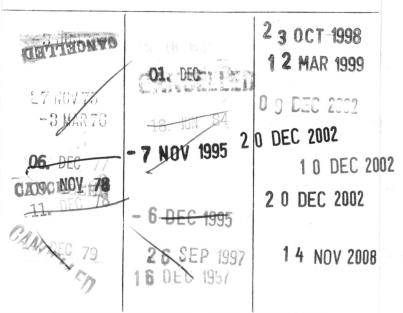
Books must be returned promptly, or renewed, on or before the last date stamped above.

FAILURE TO DO SO WILL INCUR FINES

PL/17

PROXEMIC BEHAVIOR

APPROACHES
TO
SEMIOTICS

edited by

THOMAS A. SEBEOK

assisted by

JULIA KRISTEVA · JOSETTE REY-DEBOVE

8

1970

MOUTON

THE HAGUE · PARIS

PROXEMIC BEHAVIOR

A CROSS-CULTURAL STUDY

by

O. MICHAEL WATSON

1970

MOUTON

THE HAGUE · PARIS

LIBRARY OF CONGRESS CATALOG CARD NUMBER: 79-120353

Printed in The Netherlands by Mouton & Co., Printers, The Hague.

To Billy Shears

PREFACE

This book deals with that area of human behavior for which Edward T. Hall has coined the term PROXEMICS. The study of proxemic behavior is concerned with man's structuring and perception of space and includes a broad range of spatial behavior, from the structuring of small amounts of space in daily interaction to the layout of cities. Investigations of proxemic behavior have only recently been initiated and researchers in the area of proxemics have an enormous task ahead of them: the description and comparison of cross-cultural differences in the structuring and perception of space and the reasons for these differences.

The research reported in this book is an attempt at observation, description, and comparison of different, culturally specific systems of proxemic behavior under controlled conditions. Further, it deals with only a small segment of the total spectrum of behavior included within the definition of proxemics, proxemic behavior on the interpersonal level — the ways in which man relates physically to other men in structuring microspace in face-to-face interactions with other men, and the meanings attached to these relationships. It is hoped that this small step can serve as a foundation on which further empirical research can be built.

My principal acknowledgment is to Edward T. Hall, who was the first scientist to recognize and write systematically about proxemic behavior. The research reported herein is based on Dr. Hall's own work and was inspired and stimulated by his insights. Acknowledgment is also due to Drs. Theodore D. Graves, Gordon W. Hewes, Dorothea V. Kaschube, and Gottfried O. Lang, all of whom read the manuscript and made many helpful suggestions. I also wish to extend my gratitude to my wife, Mary Jo Watson, whose tolerance of my fretful behavior during the writing of this book was truly remarkable. Finally, although it seems clumsy to thank an institution, my thanks are nevertheless due to the United States Public Health Service which provided support for this research under grants 5-T1 MH-8150-02 and 5-T1 MH-8150-03.

O.M.W.

TABLE OF CONTENTS

LIST OF TABLES

LIST OF FIGURES

I

INTRODUCTION

One inconvenience I sometimes experienced in so small
a house, is the difficulty of getting to a sufficient distance
from my guest when we began to utter the big thoughts
in big words. You want room for your thoughts to
get into sailing trim and run a course or two before they
make their port... Individuals, like nations, must have
suitable broad and natural boundaries, even a considerable
neutral ground, between them. I have found it a singular
luxury to talk across the pond to a companion on the
opposite side. In my house we were so near that we could
not begin to hear — could not speak low enough to be
heard... If we are merely loquacious and loud talkers,
then we can afford to stand very near together, cheek by
jowl, and feel each other's breath; but if we speak reserved-
ly and thoughtfully we want to be farther apart, that
all animal heat and moisture may have a chance to evapo-
rate... As the conversation began to assume a loftier and
grander tone, we gradually shoved our chairs farther apart
till they touched the wall in opposite corners, and then
commonly there was not room enough.

Henry D. Thoreau, *Walden*

The United States is a nation of tourists, and in their travels Americans
come into contact with people from different cultures whose behavior
they often find so strange as to defy interpretation. Traveling in
Mediterranean Europe, and trying to interact with natives of that area,
the tourists feel intimidated by the aggressive behavior they encounter:
the close conversational distance, the high voice level, and the inordinate
amount of touching during a conversation. American visitors to the Near
East are shocked, surprised, and outraged to see Arab men holding hands
in public. Even in their own country Americans come across puzzling
behavior: they are struck by the apparent shyness of the Navaho Indians,
who speak in a voice so quiet as to be barely audible and avoid direct eye
contact. These tourists are examples of people who have observed, and

often been made uncomfortable by, differences in proxemic behavior.

Proxemics is the study of the ways in which humans structure and use space. The term 'proxemics' evokes an image of proximity, and Edward T. Hall, innovator of the term and pioneer in the study of proxemic behavior, chose it "... because it suggests the subject to the reader" (Hall, 1963b: 1022). Hall (1963b: 1003) defines proxemics as "... the study of how man unconsciously structures microspace — the distance between men in conduct of daily transactions, the organization of space in his houses and buildings, and ultimately the layout of his towns." In a later article, Hall (1964: 41) defines proxemics in a way which emphasizes the importance of the communicative process in proxemics: "... the study of ways in which man gains knowledge of the content of other men's minds through judgments of behavior patterns associated with varying degrees of proximity to them." Most recently, Hall (1966: 1) writes that proxemics is "... the interrelated observations and theories of man's use of space as a specialized elaboration of culture." Hall includes within these definitions of proxemics a wide range of spatial behavior in man from a personal, transactional level through architecture to city planning, and the structuring of space as a communicative device. Although the total range of proxemic behavior is wide, this book is concerned primarily with the personal transactional level of proxemic behavior as a system of nonverbal communication: how man perceives and utilizes small amounts of space in face-to-face interactions with other men.

In a cross-cultural context, what would be perceived as a close distance for a conversation by a North American might be normal for an Arab or Latin American. Hall (1955) reports some interesting, and often amusing, incidents which illustrate cross-cultural differences in the structuring of space. Latin Americans, for instance, feel that North Americans maintain a greater distance during conversations than is normal in Latin America. North Americans, on the other hand, feel that Latins are too 'pushy' because they converse at distances which are thought to be too close in the United States. North American businessmen in Latin America barricade themselves behind desks to keep their Latin associates at a comfortable conversational distance. When confronted with this frustrating barrier to a normal business transaction, Latin Americans have been known to eschew dignity and attempt to climb over or around the desk.

Actual distance is not the only dimension which works to give a feeling of closeness or distance. Such factors as the degree of directness with which one person faces another, eye contact, touching, voice loudness, olfaction, and detection of body heat also play an important part in proxemic behavior. Southeast Asians do not ordinarily touch each other during a conversation, and touching on the head is a serious breach of etiquette. People in the United States raise their voices to make a point, not necessarily in anger, while among the Chinese raising the level of the voice is characteristically associated with anger and loss of self-control. Arabs use their eyes in a conversation more than Americans do. Foreign visitors to the United States often express dismay at the American practice of putting feet up on desks or tables, and mention that to do the same in their countries would be extremely impolite and disrespectful.

The examples cited above serve to point out that when people from different cultures interact, they cannot be relied upon to attach the same meanings to the same elements of proxemic behavior. When two systems of proxemic behavior clash "... there [is] interference between two patterns, or a perceived absence of patterning, during an encounter" (Hall, 1963b: 1005). The interference resulting when proxemic elements from different cultures meet, in this case Arab and American, is well illustrated by a quote from Hall (1963b: 1005): "Americans were not only aware of uncomfortable feelings, but the intensity and the intimacy of the encounter with Arabs was likely to be anxiety provoking. The Arab look, touch, voice level, the warm moisture of his breath, the penetrating stare of his eyes, all proved to be disturbing."

In his writings Hall has provided a useful and insightful framework in which to view proxemic behavior. He has isolated the elements which form the system of proxemic behavior and has provided a method for their notation (1963b). His work serves as a guide for empirical study and provides a background for the interpretation of these data.

Research has been done (Watson and Graves, 1966) utilizing the system of notation for proxemic behavior provided by Hall (1963b) in an attempt to empirically quantify reports of the differences in Arab and American proxemic behavior. The results strikingly validated Hall's (1963b) impressions: "... Arabs confronted each other more directly than Americans when conversing..., they sat closer to each other..., they looked each other more squarely in the eye..., they conversed more loudly than Americans ... and NO OVERLAPPING is to be found between the distribution of mean scores within the Arab subgroups and within American subgroups" (Watson and Graves, 1966: 977). This research found not only significant differences in Arab and American proxemic behavior, but also found the system of notation for proxemic behavior (Hall, 1963b) to be practicable. The relatively small sample size (16 Arabs and 16 Americans) and gross ethnic differences of the two groups put certain limits on general statements about proxemic behavior, however.

One of the objectives of the present research was to record proxemic behavior of a larger sample of male foreign students studying at the University of Colorado. These subjects represented countries from all over the world, and observations provided a broad range of empirical data on proxemic behavior in a laboratory setting. An attempt was then made to proxemically classify geographic areas on the basis of these data.

Another aim of this research was to test the pertinence of the categories provided by Hall (1963b) for the systematization of proxemic behavior. Subjects were interviewed in an attempt to determine whether these categories are the only important ones operable in a cross-cultural context, or if other dimensions of proxemic behavior can be uncovered. Subjects were also interviewed as to the proxemic differences which they may have encountered in the United States or in other foreign countries. This is an attempt to get at the meanings attached to proxemic norms.

Very little is known about how proxemic behavior is transmitted and learned. Subjects have been queried for explicit rules which might exist in their culture, or for evidence of learning proxemic patterns by imitation. These are attempts to uncover insights as to how people incorporate proxemic behavior into their behavioral repertoire.

Finally, an attempt has been made to measure the effect of Western, industrial cultures on the proxemic behavior of other areas of the world. This was done by means of a questionnaire subjects were required to complete, which supplies information concerning urban experience and foreign travel.

In the next chapter a brief survey is made of the evidence of the importance of spatial behavior in animals and in man, and each category of proxemic behavior isolated by Hall (1963b) is discussed more fully. Chapter III concerns itself with methodology, discussing the research design and aims of the research. Data analysis is discussed in Chapter IV and the findings of the research are presented. Chapter V puts proxemic behavior in a theoretical framework as a form of non-verbal communication. The final chapter presents a summary and conclusions of the research, and suggestions for further research in proxemics.

II

THE STRUCTURING OF SPACE IN ANIMALS AND MAN

This chapter is divided into two major sections, the first of which deals with the structuring of space in non-human animals, primarily mammals. The importance of territoriality is briefly demonstrated, followed by a discussion of the ways in which animals regulate distances among themselves. Finally, the behavioral and physiological disruptions which occur when animals are forced to live in overcrowded conditions are described. The second major section is concerned with man and his structuring of space, starting with territorial behavior and crowding in man. Then, man's use of his senses in the perception of space is discussed, followed by a section concerned with the ways in which culture modifies man's use of space. Finally, each variable which Hall (1963b) includes in his system of proxemic behavior is dealt with.

SPATIAL BEHAVIOR IN ANIMALS

Introduction

There is a gap, a kind of 'no man's land', which exists between the biological and the social sciences, but there seems to be a growing consensus that the study of animal behavior carefully applied to man can lead to new insights and new directions of research in the sciences of man. Hediger (1961: 36), a pioneer in the study of animal psychology, writes: "... human behavior can never be understood as something isolated, but only in its phylogeny as revealed by comparative studies." Others agree that the phylogenetic point of view is helpful in applying generalizations about animal behavior to that of man (Davis, 1962: 316; Tinbergen, 1952: 22). Hall (1963a: 424, 1966: ix) reminds us that man's culture transcends him in time and space and that much of his behavior is rooted in his phylogenetic past. Man is, Hall (1966: ix) writes, "first, last, and always, like other members of the animal kingdom, a prisoner of his biological organism.... The more we learn about animals and the intricate adaptive mechanisms evolution has produced, the more relevant these studies become to the solution of some of the more baffling human problems." Davis (1962: 316) agrees that "a knowledge of the biological origin or history of many human problems has often stimulated research and produced understanding...". Buettner-Janusch (1966: 190) is also of the opinion that much about man can be learned from an examination of the behavior of his relatives, but cautions that, since man has diverged radically from other animals in his evolution, one must be careful not to construct false analogies. However, many valuable data from sub-human animals can be used to make deductions in a metaphorical as well as a direct way. Hall (1966: 7) further points out that animal studies are valuable because the relatively short animal generations allow us to observe direction, extent, and rate of change in a way which would be impossible in man. Also, humans have culture, by means of which they often obscure issues and rationalize behavior, which other animals do not.

This review of spatial behavior in animals obviously is not an attempt to 'bridge the gap' between biological and social science. It is, rather, a brief presentation of the recently acquired knowledge of the importance of the structuring of space in animals. It is followed by sections dealing with interesting parallels in man.

Territoriality

The song "Born Free" won the 1966 Academy Award for "Best Song from a Motion Picture". It exemplifies the saccharin, sentimental popular notion of animal behavior. The phrase "Free as a Bird" is another good example of this attitude. Animals are NOT born free to roam the world at will, and most cling tenaciously to the area of land, air, or water with which they are intimately acquainted, and within which they live their lives.

A brief review of some animal studies concerned with territoriality is presented in this section in order to demonstrate how some animals possess and defend territory, and what are some important functions and consequences of territoriality.

It has been known since the early part of the 17th century that some animals possess and defend territory (Carpenter, 1958: 224-225), but it was not until 1920, when Eliot Howard published *Territory in Bird Life*, that a single work was devoted exclusively to the study of territoriality.

The earlier works mentioning territoriality were written primarily about birds, but it is now known that many other animals besides birds exhibit territorial behavior, and the study of territoriality is now becoming a regular part of field studies of animals (Carpenter, 1958: 228). The study of territorial behavior in animals is even becoming a discipline in itself, and Hediger (1961: 34) suggests that it be called 'territorology'.

A species occupies a primary topographical unit called a 'biotope' (Hediger, 1950: 6-7). The biotope of a species is further subdivided into 'home ranges'. The home range is that section of the biotope which a group of animals, or an individual animal, normally utilizes in the search for food. Home ranges usually overlap, and this area of overlap is neutral ground to the species involved (Burt, 1943: 351). Some animals divide the home range into even smaller sections, a protected place called a home site or, more commonly, a territory. A territory is an area of space which an individual animal, a pair of animals, or an animal group possesses exclusively and is defended, usually by the male, against in-intruders of the same species (Ardrey, 1966: 3; Hediger, 1950: 6-7, 1961: 36). Hediger (1955: 17) notes that the territories of animals of different species overlap and even coincide, but the territories of animals of the same species are mutually exclusive, occupying separate areas of space, like tiles in a mosaic. Hediger (1955: 17-18) also reports that the size of a territory is based on the abundance of the food supply, territorial needs usually being largest where there is a scarcity of food and smallest in captivity where an ample food supply is assured. The territory of some animals is defined in time as well as space (Carpenter, 1935: 175; Lorenz, 1966: 35). Two territories may overlap in space, but the animals occupying the territories avoid conflict by using the overlap on a different time schedule. Territoriality, then, is a system "whereby animals distribute living space and food supplies..." (Clark, 1962: 179).

In general, territoriality can be looked upon as a means of relating the needs of animals to the environment (Davis, 1962: 317), and Carpenter (1958: 242-243), in his excellent review article on territorial behavior, lists 32 inferences of the functions of territoriality which he has culled from the literature of animal studies. Some functions seem to be more important, and are mentioned more frequently than others, and these will be discussed briefly below.

First of all, territoriality spreads an animal population evenly throughout its biotope. It serves the function of regulating population dispersal and seems, indirectly perhaps, to regulate population numbers (Carpenter, 1958: 244). Errington (1956: 306) has observed that territoriality is a 'self-limiting' device in animal populations, and, in animals without territory, something outside the population usually acts as a limiting agent. For example, animals which have not established a territory, or have lost it, are more vulnerable to predation than animals which have a territory (Errington, 1938: 190). Wynne-Edwards (1965: 1543) also mentions the importance of territoriality as a mechanism for the self-regulation of animal populations. The dispersal of an animal population over a wide area also prevents the presentation of a large, concentrated target for predators (Michelmore, 1964: 174). Dispersal also reduces mortality in an animal population through the reduction of the spread of disease (Burt, 1949: 26). The elimination or reduction of parasites is also achieved by dispersal through territoriality (Carpenter, 1958: 243). Establishing and holding a territory is a life or death matter in most cases, and thus has a definite survival value. Territoriality also serves as an intermediate factor between an animal population and its food supply (Carpenter, 1958: 244). Overcrowded conditions may lead to a lack of food (Michelmore, 1964: 174). Burt (1943: 350) also links territory to the food supply. The importance of the linkage of territory and food supply is attested to by the fact that, in animals which exhibit territorial behavior, "... starvation, when we observe it, tends to be a sporadic or accidental cause of mortality rather than a regular one" (Wynne-Edwards, 1965: 1544). Burt (1949: 26) has pointed out that in a non-territorial species a local population can build to such proportions that the food supply can be exhausted in a short time, leading to starvation.

Territoriality and sexual behavior are also linked. "Territorial behavior is designed to prevent loss of contact among reproducing units" (Hediger, 1961: 37). Territoriality allows animals to reproduce and rear their young (Burt, 1943: 350; Carpenter, 1958: 244). Birds which do not establish a territory, for example, do not reproduce (Wynne-Edwards, 1965: 1544). Individuals which are excluded from a territory do not usually reproduce and do not, therefore, contribute genetically to the population and are thus evolutionary failures (Carpenter, 1958: 244).

There is a linkage between territoriality and agonistic behavior, for, combined with social organization, it "reduces stress, conflict, pugnacity, and nonadaptive expenditure of energy" (Carpenter, 1958: 245). The stabilization of stimulus contacts, through territoriality, thus reduces agonistic behavior (Clark, 1962: 179). Michelmore (1964: 45) reports that the sight of copulating animals arouses aggression in animals of the same species. The possession of a territory allows animals some degree of privacy from the prying eyes of their fellows and reduces aggression in this way. Territoriality generally controls fighting simply by keeping strange animals apart (Scott, 1962: 169).

All of the functions of territoriality mentioned above are important in maintaining optimal conditions of population stability, and "an optimal dynamic stability of a population is a favorable condition for species survival..." (Carpenter, 1958: 244-245).

Carpenter (1958: 245) writes that "it may be hypothesized that physical-geographical changes which radically disturb the territorial order of a species population may seriously and adversely affect the survival of the species." Schjelderup-Ebbe (reported in Allee, 1958: 141) found, for example, that chickens in their own home yard win more fights than do strangers to the yard. It has been observed that the closer to the center of its territory an animal is, the more confident and aggressive it becomes (Lorenz, 1966: 35). When an animal is in its own territory, it is provided with security for defense and is provided with a psychological advantage which favorably affects motivation (Carpenter, 1958: 243). In studies on canaries Shoemaker (1939: 381-406) found that a particular bird, even though it ranked low in the neutral ground around the bath bowls, feeding places, or nesting material storage areas, was dominant in the territory it had established. Birds lowest in the social order dominate the area around their nesting cages.

Buettner-Janusch (1966: 238) writes that field studies have shown that animals make every effort to remain in their own territories, and become uneasy when they leave the familiar confines of the territory. Clark (1962: 182) reports heightened excitability in mice caused by the disruption of the customary territory of the animal. Zoo animals "feel comfortable and safe only in their territory. If they are forcibly removed, disturbances are unavoidable..." (Hediger, 1955: 117). Hediger (1955: 115) says further that wild animals are fixed to space, and an adult wild animal in a zoo, moved to another area, may not survive the shock. All indications are that 'feeling at home' is more than an idle phrase.

Although territorial behavior has wide variation in different species, it is "nevertheless almost universally exhibited in some form from the fishes through the primates. It would seem, therefore, that it has important relationships to the adaptive, selective, and survival mechanisms of animal evolution" (Carpenter, 1958: 244). It appears that there are many more animals which display territorial behavior than those which do not. Some animals have territory during only a limited time, during breeding seasons, for example (Hediger, 1961: 34), but most animals exhibit permanent territorial behavior. Although the widest distribution of territoriality is among the vertebrates, some invertebrates have it (Burt, 1943: 346). The octopus confines its activity to a circumscribed area and behaves aggressively toward other octopi entering this area (Dethier and Stellar, 1961: 39). Some insects defend a given piece of ground as a territory and are able to orient to it from a distance (Dethier and Stellar, 1961: 42). Even the lowly planarium, a worm which lacks brain, blood, and rectum seems to display a crude semblance of territorial behavior by 'preferring' to eat in places with which it is 'familiar' (Best and Rubinstein, 1962: 916-918).

Altmann (1962:277) lists territoriality as one of the major features of vertebrate social behavior, and it occurs, in some form or another, in all classes of vertebrates (Errington, 1938: 195, 1956: 305; Hediger, 1961: 34). In fishes, it has been observed in cichlids, sunfish, bream, char (Carpenter, 1958: 230-231), and sticklebacks (Dethier and Stellar, 1961: 73; Tinbergen, 1952: 24). Among reptiles it has been observed in some lizards and turtles (Carpenter, 1958: 232). Birds have been known to display territorial behavior for a long time (Carpenter, 1958: 232-235; Hediger, 1955: 82; Howard, 1920). The territorial principle has also been found to be valid for most mammals (Hediger, 1955: 82). Among the rodents which have territoriality are beavers, many species of squirrels, cotton tail rabbits, many rats and mice, and prairie dogs (Carpenter, 1958: 235-237). It had been assumed that no species of deer defended territory, but it has been found that this is not true (Ardrey, 1966: 83-87; Carpenter, 1958: 238-240). Eskimo dogs defend territory (Michelmore, 1964: 177; Tinbergen, 1951: 150), as do wolves (Mowat, 1963: 89).

Primates exhibit territorial behavior, and Carpenter (1958: 242) concludes that it is as characteristic of primates as of other vertebrates. Lemurs are aware of territorial boundaries (Buettner-Janusch, 1966: 231, 238), and Jolly (1966: 143) maintains that "all the social Lemuroidea have sharply localized, stable home ranges and territories." Field studies on monkeys have demonstrated that territoriality exists among them also. Carpenter (1934: 43-55) reports that Howler monkeys are strongly territorial, as are red spider monkeys (1935: 175). Capuchin monkeys also possess and defend a territory (Buettner-Janusch, 1966: 251). Baboons appear to be territorial in that they know their territory quite well (Buettner-Janusch, 1966: 274), but Washburn and Devore (1961a: 93, 1961b: 63), in their field studies, have noticed areas of overlap of neighboring troops, and prefer to say that baboons have only a home range. When different troops had contact with each other they did so without mixing, although members of the troops might be only a few feet from each other.

Carpenter (1940: 152-164), in field studies in Thailand, found territoriality to be a fundamental characteristic of behavior in the gibbon, although their territories, like those of baboons, were often found to overlap. Schaller (1965: 221) found that Highland gorilla bands shared their range with others of their kind, but when strangers were met they usually ignored each other. Perhaps the fact that food resources were abundant had something to do with the lack of strong territorial behavior in gorillas, for it has been observed that baboons display stronger territorial behavior when the food supply is less abundant (Buettner-Janusch, 1966: 274). Although gorillas do not display strong territorial behavior, Schaller (1965: 210-211) reports that there appeared to be certain boundaries beyond which a gorilla group would not roam. As the young gorillas grew up they learned not only the more obvious aspects of the home range but also its finest features. Perhaps, as more and more primate studies are made, an effort to alleviate the ambiguity of 'territory' and 'home range' in the higher primates will be made.

In vertebrates a great deal of the fighting which takes place among animals of the same species is connected with territoriality (Scott, 1962: 168). Male sticklebacks select a territory in response to the sight of green vegetation and must defend it against all male intruders before they build a nest (Dethier and Stellar, 1961: 73; Tinbergen, 1952: 24). Song sparrows defend their territory by threats and fights (Davis, 1962: 317). Eskimo dogs vigorously defend territory. Young dogs constantly violate territory and are dealt severe punishment for their transgressions, but when they have matured they have learned to defend their territory and to avoid that of others (Tinbergen, 1951: 150). Sea birds have evolved an elaborate threat display with which they defend their claims from other birds (Michelmore, 1964: 176-177).

It seems that animals would constantly be blundering into another's territory and thus be constantly fighting. This would probably be true were it not for mechanisms which animals have evolved for the demarcation of their territories. Territories "are clearly defined by a variety of factors (optical, acoustic, olfactory, or various combinations of these)" (Hediger, 1950: 7). Parkes and Bruce (1961: 1049-1054) point out that birds, in general, rely on vision to play a major part in the responses to their environment, while most mammals depend on olfaction. Many mammals have special odoriferous glands with which they mark their territories. These glands are found in many different parts of the anatomy, depending on the species (Parkes and Bruce, 1961: 1053). Scent glands in deer and antelope, for example, are found above the eyes (Hediger, 1955:

19). Animals which employ the olfactory method of marking their territories leave their scent on rocks, trees, branches, etc. (Hediger, 1955: 19). The importance of olfactory communication in some animals is attested to by Hediger's (1955: 19) observations that an animal introduced into confinement with a strange animal of the same species will search the area with its nose, looking for demarcation points. Only when the area becomes familiar olfactorily will the new animal look at the other. Some animals have demarcation scent present in their excrement. Wolves, for instance, use urine to mark their territory (Mowat, 1963: 89).

The lower end of the primate scale also uses olfaction to detect marking, but the upper end uses acoustic means (Hediger, 1961: 39-40). Jolly (1966: 32) comments that "prosimians stand out among primates for the wealth and variety of their olfactory communication." Although lemurs have specialized glands for marking (Jolly, 1966: 132), they also utilize acoustic means, i.e., they vocalize (Buettner-Janusch, 1966: 238). Howler monkey troops, when meeting at the boundaries of their territories, assert their territorial rights by loudly vocalizing (Beuttner-Janusch, 1966: 254; Carpenter, 1934: 54). Indeed, they get their name from this behavior. Gibbons also vocalize in defending their territories (Buettner-Janusch, 1966: 283; Carpenter, 1940: 152-164; La Barre, 1954: 57). La Barre (1954: 169) states that when a band of gibbons meets another band at the edge of their territories they use a cry which ranges from pseudo-angry to murderous, but with no open belligerency. La Barre (1954: 169) sees this vocalization as a "symbolic substitution for action...", and compares it to human diplomacy with the function of establishing title to a territory by a politico-economic treaty. Schaller (1965: 221) has mentioned that when Highland gorillas meet a strange group the interactions are peaceful, and Kortland (1962: 131) observed that chimpanzees seldom made any noise, but "generally communicated by gesture, or by changes in posture or facial expression." Perhaps the apparent lack of territorial marking in some higher primates is part of what appears to be a rather weak territoriality in general.

Besides demarcating the boundaries of their territories, animals also structure them internally. The roaming of an animal "... does not in fact occur even in the limited section of the field we call territory, nor is this individual living space of the animal homogeneous, but highly differentiated" (Hediger, 1950: 12). Hediger (1955: 18) later writes that animals divide their territories into sleeping areas, bathing areas, and food storage areas. Certain features in an animal's territory are important. Termite nests which zebras use in grooming or the wallowing holes of red deer are examples (Hediger, 1955: 18). Hediger (1955: 19) has also found that there exists a strong tradition of spatial patterns in animals, and uses the example of ancient salt licks to illustrate this point. Animals live in a pattern of fixed points at which they perform definite functions at definite times, and use certain favorite paths in their wanderings to and from these points (Hediger, 1955: 20). Howard (1920: 9) observed: "By repetition certain performances become stereotyped, certain paths fixed, and a routine is thus established which becomes increasingly definite as the season advances."

Regulation of Distance in Animal Populations

Enemy avoidance, Hediger (1955: 51) writes, is "the primitive impulse of every healthy creature to preserve life...", and usually consists of a "... sudden and effective change of place...", i.e., running away. An animal will flee when a potential enemy approaches to a certain distance. The distance at which flight reaction occurs is called by Hediger (1955: 123) the 'flight distance', and seems to be directly proportional to an animal's size. Thus an antelope will flee from an enemy at about 500 yards, and a wall lizard at six feet (Hall, 1966: 10). An animal born in captivity has a flight distance considerably less than his feral fellows, and an adult wild animal brought to a zoo must modify its flight distance in order not to be constantly panicked by the proximity of man and other animals in the zoo (Hediger, 1955: 123). Hediger (1955: 126-127) has found that an animal reared in captivity goes through stages in modifying its flight reaction. A young animal is usually afraid of man and attempts to maintain a distance between man and itself. As the animal approaches puberty in man's company it usually loses its flight reaction in regard to man. But with maturity there is again a tendency to keep a distance from man. This final transformation, Hediger maintains, has nothing to do with flight reaction, but with social organization. The animal has organized itself with others of the same species and stands in a complex relationship with them in a group, and regards man with a particular kind of animosity, as man has no place in the animals' social order. Hediger (1950: 34) states that flight distances in animals can be accurately measured, and presents a table listing flight distances of various animals.

Related to flight distance is critical distance. Everyone has heard that a cornered animal will fight, but this is not entirely accurate. A cornered animal probably will not fight if allowed enough space. A critical distance, according to Hediger (1955: 124-125), is that distance at which flight reaction changes, i.e., when an animal changes from flight to attack. If an animal is cornered and an enemy oversteps the critical distance, the animal will then begin the attack. Hediger (1955: 124-125) presents a very interesting illustration of lion and tiger tamers judging the flight and critical distances very accurately, and will approach the animal and cause it to retreat from the man. When the animal is in a position from which it cannot retreat farther, e.g., in the corner of its cage, the trainer will overstep the animal's critical distance, causing the animal to take defensive measures. The animal will slowly and deliberately stalk the trainer while he is within critical distance, often climbing over obstacles in its path, advancing in a straight line towards the trainer. By putting obstacles of his choice in the animal's path, stools or pedestals for instance, the trainer lets the animal stalk him until it is on one of the obstacles, then quickly steps out of the area of critical distance, which leaves the animal on the pedestal or stool. The results are highly successful, or, in the jargon of show business, 'we've got a hit on our hands'. In this context the jodhpurs, riding boots, pith helmet, chair, and whip that most lion tamers use are largely unnecessary as far as the animals are concerned, but seem to have a positive effect on the audience at a circus.

Flight distance and critical distance are maintained by animals in interactions between members of different species. Some categories of distance regulation have also been observed when members of the same species interact. Hediger (1950: 111, 1955: 66) has observed two distinct categories in vertebrates, 'contact' and 'non-contact' species. A contact species not only tolerates close physical contact by accident, but deliberately seeks such contact. Contact animals "arrange things so as to get into closest possible contact with members of their species" (Hediger, 1955: 66). These animals are also fond of being stroked and fondled. A non-contact species will "avoid close contact with animals of the same species. Tame members of this group withdraw before the human hand, and dislike being stroked or scratched" (Hediger, 1955: 66). It is obvious, however, that a non-contact animal has contact under certain conditions, such as sexual activity and rearing the young. No particular reason has yet been found as to why certain species fall into one or the other of these categories, as animals which are closely related may belong to different groups (Hall, 1965: 14, 1966: 12). Examples of contact species include wild boars, hedgehogs, owls, tortoises, many primates, and, incredibly enough, porcupines. Representatives of the non-contact group are cats, dogs (apparently the less well domesticated varieties), flamingoes, doves, gulls, starlings, swallows, and many ruminants (Hediger, 1955: 66). The Adelie penguin, a non-contact species, had a more limited range than the Emperor penguin, which is a contact animal. By huddling together, and thus conserving body heat, the Emperor ranges into the colder parts of Antarctica, where the Adelie penguin probably could not survive (Hall, 1965: 14, 1966: 12). Hall (1966: 12) suggests that contact species are more 'involved' with each other and that perhaps their social organization and exploitation of their environment might be different from non-contact species. It would seem, Hall (1966: 12) goes on, that non-contact species might be more vulnerable to the stress of crowding.

Animals also maintain certain other distances in intra-species interaction, which vary according to the species. These are individual, or personal, distance and social, or group, distance. Hediger first applied the term 'individual distance' to animals in 1941. Individual distance is that distance which non-contact animals normally maintain between themselves and other individuals of the same species (Hediger, 1950: 111). This distance is like "an invisible bubble that surrounds the organism" (Hall, 1966: 12). This 'bubble' moves with the animal, has no topographical reference, and into which no other individual is normally permitted entrance (Condor, 1949: 651). Birds evenly spaced along a telephone wire are an example of individual distance which is readily observable. Individual distance, then, "denotes the minimum distance within which individuals may approach each other" (Hediger, 1955: 83).

Individual distance sometimes varies in an animal, e.g., when a Black-headed gull searches for food its individual distance is greater than it is at other times (Condor, 1949: 649). Individual distance is also a factor interrelated with social organization (Hall, 1966: 12-13). Allee (1958:135) reports experiments with chickens which have demonstrated that the more dominant bird, when two birds were released from behind transparent doors in full sight of each other, traveled farther toward the less dominant one. Position in the social order could be inferred by the relative distance each bird traveled. Similar observations of the correlation of individual distance and social rank have been reported for many birds and mammals (Hall, 1966: 13).

Social distance is utilized by animals to keep in touch with the group. Social distance is "the maximum distance between individuals of any group..." (Hediger, 1955: 83). Washburn and DeVore (1961b: 62) write: "Most of a baboon's life is spent within a few feet of other baboons. The troop affords protection from predators and an intimate group knowledge of the territory it occupies." It is therefore critically important that an animal keep in contact with the group. A lost baboon is a dead baboon. Hall (1966: 13) writes that it is "not simply the contact with his group — that is, the distance at which it can no longer see, hear, or smell the group — it is rather a psychological distance, one at which the animal apparently begins to feel anxious when he exceeds its limits. We can think of it as a hidden band that CONTAINS the group." This 'hidden band' varies from species to species. A pack of howler monkeys, for example, is more compact than one of spider monkeys, i.e., spider monkeys display a greater social distance (Hediger, 1955: 83). Social distance varies within a species in certain situations also. In times of danger a group is more compact (Hall, 1966: 14). Social distance has been reported with some frequency among vertebrates "from the fish to the gorilla" (Hediger, 1961: 54).

Overcrowding

It has been known for some time that crowding is almost always harmful to animals, with the exception of animals crowding together to hibernate through the winter, to breed, or to migrate (Allee, 1958: 17-18). Hogg (1854), for example, noted that water snails, when crowded, may not grow at all and when they do grow, it is at a slower rate than their less crowded fellows. Overcrowding can even play an important role in determining the morphology of an animal. A species of South African grasshopper has two phases: the *solitaria*, which results from nymphs being raised in uncrowded conditions, and the *gregaria* phase, which is a change brought about by crowding (Allee, 1934). Whether or not a fertilized bee or wasp egg will produce a worker or a reproductive female (a 'queen') depends on space and food. If the egg receives enough food and is given plenty of space in which to grow, the result will likely be a sexually mature female; if less well fed and more crowded, a worker will hatch (Allee, 1958: 167). Studying a species of *moina*, a 'water flea', it was found that crowding produced environmental stress. Eggs have a different prospective potency than those produced by females in uncrowded conditions (Allee, 1934: 30-34).

The writings of Malthus relate population to the food supply, but it has been only recently that research has indicated that predation and food are not the only factors which interact with population size (Hall, 1966: 17). Errington (1956: 307) mentioned that too little attention had been paid to the importance of the self-controlling mechanisms which play a part in population dynamics. Wynne-Edwards (1965: 1543-1544) has written that populations tend to stabilize even in the absence of predators, and further points out that starvation is sporadic or accidental. John Calhoun (1952: 139) feels that the subject of population dynamics is commonly treated from a demographic point of view which emphasizes that population dynamics are dependent upon the interrelationship of birth, death, and migration to determine the population density. In the study of these factors attention is given to the abundance of food, health of the general population, and climatic conditions. Calhoun maintains that not enough attention is paid to the role of the individual or to the internal workings of the individual's social group. It will be demonstrated that the effects of crowding of individual animals, even with ample food and absence of predators, can have, in turn, drastic effects on the population.

A summary of the work of John Christian and his associates (1960: 79-95) will be given, because of the important implications of the research and because Christian had the rare opportunity to observe population collapse in a natural environment. Christian did his research on James Island in the Chesapeake Bay on a herd of Sika deer which had been breeding freely over a period of several years. When he began his work in 1955 there were about 300 deer in the population. Christian shot five deer and gave them detailed autopsies and recorded the results. No change in the population occurred during the next two years, but in the early part of 1958 over half of the deer population suddenly died. The next year more deer died, and the population leveled out at about 80 animals. During the period of die-off and stabilization Christian collected a dozen carcasses for study. It should be noted here that there was no predation and ample food on the island. Histological studies of the deer collected from the die-off were healthy, like the deer which were earlier shot for a control group, but Christian found that the victims of the population collapse differed in one respect from the control group. That was in the size of the adrenal glands, which were 28 to 34% heavier than the adrenals of the control group. Carcasses taken after the population stabilized showed an 81% decrease in adrenal weight. The adrenal glands taken from the die-off carcasses showed cellular changes which indicated death due to stress. Adrenals are not fixed in weight, but respond to stress. When an animal is stressed too much the adrenals respond by enlarging (Hall, 1966: 19). The deer, it seems, literally died of shock brought about by the stress of crowding. Selye (1956) has also pointed out that animals can die of shock if stressed repeatedly.

As Christian has vividly demonstrated the physiological entropy caused by overcrowding, Calhoun (1952, 1956, 1962a, 1962b) has shown how the social organization and behavior of an overcrowded population can be disrupted. Speaking of house mice, Calhoun (1956: 102) showed that "as population density increases, continued disruptions of homeostasis can transform a genetically determined stable physiology into a phenotypic unstable physiology with all the accompanying alterations in behavior." These "alterations in behavior" are lucidly presented by some experiments Calhoun (1962b) did with Norway rats. Over a period of many months Calhoun observed the population growth which occurred when he introduced five pregnant Norway rats into a quarter acre outdoor pen. He controlled variables which are normally factors in the rats' wild state by eliminating predation and amply feeding the rats. Even under these conditions the population stabilized at about 150 individuals and never exceeded 200, although physically there was enough room for more rats. Calhoun also found that the rats organized themselves in a dozen groups of twelve individuals each and noted that this was the maximum limit of group membership with maintenance of harmonious living.

With the discovery that the rat population would stabilize even though food supply and predation were controlled, Calhoun designed indoor experiments in which populations of rats were allowed to build up freely and were observed without disturbance. He then observed what conditions crowding could bring about. The living space for the rats consisted of four 5' × 7' rooms, each room being connected to the next by a ramp with the exception of the first and last rooms in the series, which were not connected to each other. Each room had a food and water supply. Calhoun introduced one or two pregnant rats into each of the pens. The ramps were removed and the young rats were allowed to mature. Calhoun maintained a balanced sex ratio by removing excess rats, leaving a total of 32 rats. The ramps were then replaced and the rats were allowed to explore the pens. The second series of pens began with 56 rats.

Calhoun then did nothing but remove the excess infants in order to keep the population at a maximum of 80 rats, which was twice the number at which stress could be detected. Calhoun feared that if the rats were allowed to multiply freely the population would suffer a collapse (like the deer on James Island). He then observed the effects of stress on several generations of rats.

Two dominant male rats occupied the end pens with a group of eight to ten females. The middle pens were occupied by the remaining 14 male rats and the rest of the females. Calhoun fixed the food hoppers so food would take a long period of time to extract. As the population grew, the chances were less and less that rats could eat by themselves at the hoppers. More rats lived in one room than any of the other three, and the frequency of contact at the hopper in this room was so increased that the rats came to redefine the feeding situation as one of eating with other rats. Gradually the hopper in the most densely populated room came to be used for 60 to 80% of all food consumption. "The development of this atypical aggregation ... forms what I have termed a BEHAVIOR SINK" (Calhoun, 1962a: 314). The term "behavioral sink" denotes a collection of foul behavior, a "pathological togetherness", as Calhoun (1962a: 315) calls it.

Although the dominant males exhibited normal behavior, the males in the behavioral sink displayed the following distortions in normal behavior: some passive males did not participate in either fighting or sexual activity; some males were hyperactive, chasing females most of the time; some males were pansexual, trying to mount any and all rats, regardless of sex or age; some males were active mainly at night when other rats slept. Female behavior was also disrupted: those in the sink area failed to make proper nests for their young; they neglected their young so that few survived, some even being eaten by other rats.

Calhoun (1962b: 148) summarizes the chaotic conditions which resulted from his experiments by saying: "It is obvious that the behavioral repertory with which the Norway rat has emerged from the trials of evolution and domestication must break down under the social pressures generated by population density."

SPATIAL BEHAVIOR IN MAN

Introduction

The definition of proxemics given earlier includes the total behavior of man in regard to the structuring of space, from the way in which he perceives his environment in terms of space, through the structuring of his cities and his houses, to the way he uses space in his interpersonal relations. This section deals with studies over this total range of spatial behavior in man. Hall's (1966: 95-122) organizing model for the classification of proxemic behavior, which has three levels, will be utilized. The first of these levels, the INFRACULTURAL, is concerned with the spatial behavior which underlies culture and has its base in man's phylogenetic past. The PRECULTURAL level deals with man's capacity to perceive space through his senses. Finally is the MICROCULTURAL level, the structuring of space as it is modified by culture.

Infracultural Level

In Hall's (1966: 95) model the structuring of space on the infracultural level is concerned with territory and crowding in man, which is "behavioral and is rooted in man's biological past." This section takes a look at territoriality and over-crowding in man. It will be a brief look, as very little systematic work has been done in human territoriality (Carpenter, 1958: 245) or the effects of crowding in man (Hall, 1966: 161).

When man acquired the habit of hunting, which was fully developed by the middle Pleistocene, a change in his territorial habits must have taken place. Other primates require a relatively small territory to fulfill the needs of their diet, which is almost exclusively herbivorous. Once man developed as a carnivore he had to search over a much larger area than his vegetarian cousins, as his food source was highly mobile (Washburn and Avis, 1958: 434). Burt (1943: 346) asserts that territoriality reaches its highest development in humans. At the band level of human social organization, for example, "bands are frequently defined in terms of the territory that they conventionally inhabit. Often the name of the band is the name of the territory" (Service, 1962: 71). Further, a band, to hunt effectively, probably must have a familiarity with its territory (Service, 1962: 48). Tribes, too, are defined by the anthropologist on the basis of independent territorial units (Mair, 1962: 15). At the level of the modern state the importance of territory is obvious. The authority of a nation extends over its territory, which boundaries are defended against intrusion (Mair, 1962: 11-12). Ardrey (1966: 230-233) maintains that the Japanese attack on Pearl Harbor in 1941 ended the isolationist attitude of the United States as its citizens joined one another in making commitments to defend their country's territorial integrity. Ardrey (1966: 238-239) further contrasts the importance of territorial defense, as exemplified by the Battle of Britain and the Finnish thwarting of a Russian invasion in the "Winter War", to the rapid collapse of France in World War II. The British and the Finns, Ardrey argues, were nations which thought of themselves as integral territorial units. France, he continues, was not one territorial unit. Like Italy, it was a country comprised of *noyaux*, smaller territorial units within the country. Ardrey (1966: 305-312) further asserts that Israel owes its existence to Arab hostility in that the Arabs give the Israelis something to defend.

There is also private territory. "The removal of boundary markers and trespass upon the property of another man are punishable acts in much of the Western world. A man's home has been his castle in English common law for centuries..." (Hall, 1966: 9). Hall (1959: 51, 147) earlier gives some interesting anecdotal evidence of territoriality in man, using a beggar's beat, a man's 'favorite chair', and a salesman's possession and defense of his territory as examples. Anyone who is familiar with American 'Western' movies and television programs recognizes "This town ain't big enough for the both of us, stranger" as a recurring theme. Davis (1962: 319) mentions that human gangs display typically primate behavior in their territoriality. Block and Niederhoffer (1958: 168) point out that a gang defends its territory by means of a 'rumble', or inter-gang fight. German prisoners in World War II, Hall (1966: 126) reports, built partitions to separate themselves from other prisoners within their own territory. Sommer (1966) writes about how people place themselves in libraries in order to avoid others. Altman and Haythorn (1967), in experiments with volunteers, described how two men isolated in a 12' × 12' room with bunks, table, and chairs came to display territorial behavior. Their first preference was for bed, then for chairs, and then position at table. They (1967: 170) say that "... it seems that personal space factors are important correlates of social, emotional states for humans as well as for other animals." Esser et al. (1964), studying schizophrenics in a mental hospital ward, observed territorial behavior. They found that low dominance patients sometimes defend territory (1964: 37-38), that patients in a somewhat higher position in the social hierarchy do not occupy a specific territory and go pretty much where they want (1964: 43), and that a low dominance person who is non-aggressive is usually "chased around all of the available space" (1964: 43). The research was conducted, they state (1964: 43), in order to eliminate undesirable and disruptive territorial patterns by restructuring the ward. Horowitz (1963), in an article dealing with painting therapy and schizophrenics, noted that a patient just beginning painting therapy would establish a territory and not permit intrusion by the therapist until it was learned that this did not mean dominance. As rapport developed, the territory was shared, but when rapport was disturbed, the territory would be divided again. It was also noted that very disturbed patients did not allot the therapist any territory (1963: 236).

Hall (1966: 161-162) reports on the only study of the consequences of insufficient space of which he knows. It was conducted in Paris by the husband-wife team of Chombard de Lauwe. They computed several measures of crowding until they found square meters per person per unit which yielded results. When space was below eight or ten square meters they found that social and physical pathologies were twice that at ten to 14 square meters. Above 14 square meters pathologies again rose, but the Chombard de Lauwes attributed this to the upward mobility of the families with this much space who devoted most of their time to achieving their goals and gave little attention to their children. Hall (1966: 157) also points out the role of an ethnic enclave in urbanization. Enclaves serve a useful function in that they allow newcomers to the city to 'urbanize' and then move out. If the size of the enclave is limited and "membership increases at a rate greater than the capacity to turn rural peoples into city dwellers..., only two choices remain: territorial growth or overcrowding." Hall is quite right in demanding reforms in urban design to counteract the effects of a behavioral sink, mentioned earlier in connection with Calhoun's studies with Norway rats. Russell (1966: 12-14) also suggests that the findings of the effects of crowding on animals be applied to man. He cautions that the world population problem should be studied more from the point of view of living space than from that of agriculture.

Precultural Level

The precultural level in the organization of space is concerned with "the physiological base shared by all human beings, to which culture gives structure and meaning" (Hall, 1966: 95). This section deals briefly with how man uses his senses in the perception of space. Hall divides the perception of space into two categories as functions of man's senses: the distance receptors (eyes, ears, and nose) (1966: 39-47), and immediate receptors, the skin and muscles (1966:49-60).

The high level of development of sight was the last and most specialized sensory adaption in primates. Stereoscopic vision was an important concomitant to arboreal living, and was developed at the expense of olfaction (Montagu and Brace, 1965: 111). Hall (1966: 40-43) presents some interesting contrasts between visual space and auditory space which will be summarized here. It has been estimated that the eyes are probably about a thousand times more effective than the ears in picking up information. The eyes can detect a visual barrier at a great distance, but a sound barrier a quarter of a mile away is hardly perceptible to the ears. Using acoustic cues, a blind man can gather information from the center of a 100-foot circle, but with sight he could see the stars (Hall, 1966:61), a poignant reminder of the importance of vision. Carpenter and McLuhan (1960) also contrast differences in visual and acoustic space. The chief characteristic of visual space, they tell us (1960: 67), is depth. We screen out much of the world in order to pinpoint an object three dimensionally in space, but "the essential feature of sound, however, is not its location, but that it BE, that it fills space. We say 'the night shall be filled with music', just as the air is filled with fragrance, locality is irrelevant." We refer to a gasoline drum filled with fumes as "empty" because it contains nothing visible to the eye (1960: 65). While visual space has a point of focus and a background, acoustic space has no boundaries and the ear favors no direction (1960: 67). Gibson (1950) distinguishes between the visual field, which is the retinal image, and the visual world, which is how man perceives these images. According to Giedion (1960), one can infer how man has perceived visual space through the ages from his art. He divides space conceptions into three phases. The primeval stage is represented by the ancient cave painting of Spain and France, and by the Eskimo art. What distinguishes primeval art is the "complete independence and freedom of its vision... In our sense there is no above and no below. No clear distinction of separateness from an intermingling, and..., no rules of proportional size" (1960: 85). There is no background and all linear directions receive the same preference. Animals in cave paintings appear to us to be standing on their heads, but to primitive man they existed in space, not subject to the laws of gravity (1960: 86-87). The next phase came with the civilizations of Egypt and Sumer. The vertical became the important direction, with the horizontal as the natural by-product. Axis and bilateral symmetry are common in the art and architecture of the ancient Near East (1960: 87). This period was displaced at the end of the 19th century by a return to the use of space without background and a freedom from the vertical and horizontal. This is typified by artists like Klee and Kandinsky (1960: 88). Marc Chagall, with his floating figures, comes to mind too. Hall (1966: 71-83) also uses art to infer clues to the perception of space, pointing out how Western art has changed through the centuries in regard to perception.

 Olfaction is also a distance receptor, although it is certainly not as effective in primates as in other mammals. Parkes and Bruce (1961) have demonstrated the importance of olfactory communication in the reproductive processes of some animals, and coined the term 'exocrinology' (1961: 1054) to emphasize the effect it has on physiological mechanisms, or endocrinology. Olfaction plays a less important part in the gathering of information by humans, although it is reported that psychiatrists can sometimes distinguish a schizophrenic from a non-schizophrenic on the basis of smell, and skilled therapists can detect the smell of anger in patients (Hall, 1966: 46). Hall (1966: 36) makes an interesting point in maintaining that one of the consequences of the suppression of olfaction in man perhaps gives him a greater ability to withstand crowding. If humans could smell as well as some other animals he would be able to detect the emotional state of people around him, and "the psychotic would begin to drive us all mad, and the anxious would make us even more anxous." The shift from olfaction to vision in man allows him to code more complex data in larger amounts, but smell is more "deeply emotional and sensually satisfying...".

Some cultures use olfaction more than others. The large number of advertisements devoted to the suppression or alteration of the odors of the body or breath attest to the American attitude toward olfaction, and Americans are often struck by the strength and variety of olfactory cues in other countries.

Consideration will now be given to the immediate receptors, the muscles and skin. "Tactual sensitivity is probably the most primitive sensory process, appearing as tropism or thigmotaxis in the lowest organism" (Frank, 1960: 5). Tactile modes of communication are also the most elemental, according to Frank (1957: 199). A young mammal receives tactile messages by feeling the mother's heartbeat through the amniotic fluid, and apparently the licking, nuzzling, and fondling of a newborn mammal by its mother has an important physiological function (Frank, 1957: 201-202). Frank (1957: 202-206, 1960: 7-9) divides the experience of human tactile communication in three phases. The first begins with birth and continues through a child's finding contact surrogates for its mother through handling blankets, toy animals, and its own body. A baby's initial orientation to space comes through tactile experience. The child explores everything within its reach by touch, until it learns that certain objects are inviolable. This restricts its tactile experience and it must learn to orient things in space by visual auditory means. The second phase begins, in our culture, around five or six years old for boys and later for girls, when they end contact with the mother. Around puberty the third phase begins with the seeking to give and receive contact. First boys walk with their arms around each other's shoulders, and girls with their arms around the waist. Then heterosexual contact is avidly sought and is manifested by 'necking' and 'petting'. Each culture, it must be emphasized, has elaborated patterns for tactile behavior. Tactile communication in sexual relations has a very highly complex code in some cultures, and other cultures have patterns of painful tactile experience, such as firewalking and scarification.

Frank (1960: 11) further asserts that much of a culture's social relations are learned and maintained through a touch code, e.g., hand shaking, hand holding, kissing, etc. Not only are codes specified for the tactile communications between persons, but also between persons and the environment, e.g., smoking, the wind blowing through one's hair, etc.

Hall (1966: 52-57) mentions the perception of thermal space as one of the skin's important functions. The skin apparently has a high capacity both to transmit and receive information concerning emotional states. This is done by temperature changes of the skin. A relatively high skin temperature enhances olfaction in that skin odors can be smelled at a greater distance. High temperatures can also make people seem more crowded than they would be in a less warm situation. The blind are particularly skilled at interpreting thermal cues, being able, for example, to navigate by means of radiated heat. *Life* magazine (1966: 106-109) has published photographs made using a system sensitive to far infrared radiation. These photographs vividly demonstrate that a person can communicate his presence after he is gone, as body heat leaves an impression which can be picked up by a thermograph and photographed. This points out that thermal radiation is not as transitory as one would think.

Microcultural Level

The microcultural level in Hall's (1966: 94-104) model deals with the structuring of space as it is modified by the effects of culture. The microcultural level has three aspects: fixed-feature, semi-fixed-feature, and informal space.

The fixed-feature aspect is, simply, those features of space which are materially fixed in the environment of a particular culture (Hall, 1966: 97). Fixed-feature space has two phases. The first of these Hall (1963a: 429) calls "internal, culturally specific". Perhaps included in this category should be the perceptual classifications which a culture makes in regard to space. In a recent book, *The Influence of Culture on Visual Perception* (Segall *et al.*, 1966: 49), it is stated "that people come to name, classify, and interpret their experiences in accord with pre-existing patterns, often linguistic, that are culturally traditional." The authors of this useful volume conclude (1966: 214) that visual perception is learned to a great extent, that "perceptions ... are determined by perceptual inference habits;

and that various inference habits are differentially likely in different societies." The Navaho language, for example, indicates that the Navaho spatial world is structured much more precisely than that of an English-speaking person (Watson, 1966). But the language may not indicate how space is materially structured. Whorf (1956: 199-200) has shown that the Hopi language is rich in the vocabulary of building components, but lacks terms which describe interior three-dimensional spaces, yet Hopi archi-tecture is rich in such spaces. Hall (1963a: 429) limits his descriptions of the internal, culturally specific phase of fixed-feature space to cross-cultural differences in the layout of cities and towns, and uses the Japanese interval system, the American grid system, and the French radiating star system as contrasting illustrations in the way cultures lay out their streets. The Japanese, in their street system, name spaces, i.e., intersections (Hall, 1959: 159, 1966: 99). Hall (1966: 142-143) relates this to the importance of intervals, or *ma*, in Japanese culture. Another interesting fact is that the Japanese number houses in the order in which they were built, not in sequence along a line (street) as we do (Hall, 1966: 99). In Anglo-Ameri-can culture edges are important (Hall, 1959: 159), and this is reflected in our street systems. We use the grid system, which originated in Asia Minor, was adopted by the Romans, and brought to England with Caesar. The grid system strings activities out (Hall, 1966: 137). The radiating star system, used in Spain and France, connects points and functions. Roads lead to the center of activity (Hall, 1966: 137). The French highway system is a series of radiating stars, the ultimate center being Paris. Hall (1966: 138) makes an interesting observation by stating that DeGaulle bases his policies on the fact that France is in a central location. Tyrwhitt (1960: 90-95), writing about the city of Fatehpur Sikri in India, points out that it is hard to find the key to the city's composition in terms of Western linear perspective. There seems to be no fixed center, but the viewer is presented with balanced panoramas from several vantage points, thus never feeling removed from the center. Hediger (1955: 20), it was mentioned above, found that animals used certain fixed paths in the course of their daily activities and compared this to humans following the same route day after day to and from work, school, etc. Lynch (1960: 47-48) found that residents of three cities in the United States consistently structured their cities into elements which Lynch calls paths, edges, districts, nodes, and land-marks. Hall (1966: 97) summarizes the internal phase of fixed-feature space by saying: "The layout of villages, towns, cities, and the intervening countryside is not haphazard but follows a plan which changes with time and culture."

We now turn to that phase of fixed-feature space which Hall (1963a: 429) calls external, environmentally fixed. This phase has to do with architecture and the layout of interior spaces. Hall (1963a: 430-435) reviews several studies dealing with the structuring of mental hospitals which seem to point out that most of these arrangements are actually non- or anti-therapeutic, aggravating patients instead of improving them. One interesting example of cross-cultural interference in architecture cited by Hall (1963a: 434) deals with a hospital built in China by Western missionaries from unaltered plans from the United States. The hospital had four stories, the first of which was the only one used with any frequency. Chinese patients were reluctant to enter it. With the Chinese Communist arrival and the expulsion of the Western administrators, the hospital was torn down and rebuilt, piece by piece, into what the Chinese considered a workable arrangement. This consisted of several separate huts, used by the patients and their families, clustered around an administrative and clinical center. Another example provided by Hall (1966: 101) is LeCorbusier's apartment building in India, the residents of which walled up the balconies provided and made them into kitchens. Hall (1966: 151) points out that Arabs do not seem to mind being crowded by people, but in their homes they want high ceilings and few walls. Hall (1966: 138) sees a similarity in the French street pattern and office arrangements: the man in charge in a French office sits in the middle, with his subordinates radiating outward. Upper middle class English men, not women, have the privacy of the bedroom and men, again not women, have dressing rooms (Hall, 1966: 133). It is surprising how our close cultural kin use the same rooms differently, but it is even more surprising to learn from Aries (1962: 390-398) that the familiar structuring of the European house into different areas for different functions, i.e., bedroom, bathroom, etc., is a fairly recent development. It was not until the 18th century that houses came to be structured the way they are now. Before that one room served as many: the bed was put up and taken down, as was the dining table. "In France and Italy", Aries (1962: 399) continues, "the word *chambre* began to be used in opposition to the word *salle* ... the *chambre* denoted the room in which one slept, the *salle* the room in which one received visitors and ate. In England the word 'room' was kept for all these functions, but a prefix was added to give precision: the diningroom, the bedroom, etc." McLuhan (1964: 124) writes: "Literate man ... tends to restrict and enclose space and to separate functions, whereas tribal man accepted his bodily functions as modes of participation in the divine energies." He (1964: 125) writes further that men lived in round houses until they became "sedentary and specialized"; then they lived in square houses. The reason, McLuhan asserts, is that the square dwelling is really the enclosure of visual space, made possible through specialization, while earlier dwellings, the round kind, are not enclosed in the visual sense, but are tactile spaces. Holzapfel-Meyer (1943: 28), quoted in English translation in Hediger (1955: 19-20) feels that to separate functions is natural for man: "The urge to occupy definite fields of activity is so obvious that we only notice it when it ceases." Schaller (1965: 198) takes exception regarding one of these natural fields of activity: "To train monkeys, apes, and men to defecate at a certain place is not at all easy, suggesting that the behavior is not a part of their natural behavioral repertoire."

The next aspect of the structuring of space on the microcultural level is semifixed-feature space. Hall (1963a: 436) defines it as "the study of furniture arrangement, screens, movable partitions and the like as factors in human interactions...". The Japanese, for example, arrange furniture in the middle of the room, while it is usually arranged along the walls in Western countries (Hall, 1966: 50). A Chinese seated on the opposite side of a desk during an interview, felt like he was on trial (Hall, 1963b: 1006). Germans do not change the position of chairs. They do not like the American habit of 'pulling up a chair'. An interesting reflection of this attitude is the famous Barcelona chair by Mies van der Rohe, a graceful piece of furniture, light and airy to look at, but almost impossible to pick up and move (Hall, 1966: 129). A useful point of reference in the study of semifixed-feature space has been provided by Osmond (1959: 7-9). He coined the term 'sociopetal' to refer to spatial arrangements which bring people together in interaction, and 'sociofugal' to refer to those which keep people apart. French side-walk cafes and American living rooms are examples of sociopetal arrangements, and waiting rooms and libraries typify sociofugal ones. More will be said about these arrangements later.

The third aspect in the structuring of space on the microcultural level is dynamic (Hall, 1963a: 429-430), or informal (Hall, 1966: 105) space. This aspect is concerned with "how man influences his communications with others by varying the spatial features of the situation" (Hall, 1963a: 430), and how "man actively USES the fixed and semifixed features given to him" (Hall, 1963a: 437). This aspect of proxemic behavior converges with the field of 'environmental' or 'ecological' psychology, i.e., the study of how man uses environmental props in his interactions (Altman and Lett, 1967; Kates and Wohlwill, 1966). More will be said below about research in this field in discussing the variables which make up the system of proxemic behavior on the interpersonal level.

Hall (1959: 163-164) lists eight distances and concomitant voice levels which Americans use in the structuring of dynamic space. Later, Hall (1964: 45-53, 1966: 109-122) elaborates on these distances and the visual, olfactory, tactile, and auditory cues which are associated with them. There are four distances, each with a close and a far phase. The first of these, intimate distance (Hall, 1966: 110-112), is characterized by a high probability of physical involvement and stepped-up sensory inputs. The close phase of intimate distance is used from wrestling and love-making, and the far phase, ranging from six to 18 inches, is generally reserved for interfamilial interactions. Personal distance (1966: 112-114), which ranges from one and a half to two and a half feet at the close phase, and two and a half to four feet at the far phase, is also used by Americans for interactions with intimates, although with less sensory involvement than at intimate distance. Social distance (1966: 114-116) is used in interacting with friends and business associates at the close phase (4 to 7 feet), and more formal business transactions at the far phase (7 to 12 feet). It should be mentioned here that the term 'social distance' is fairly commonly used in the sociological literature, but not in the same way as it is here intended. Bogardus (1933, 1959) uses the term as a measure of the degree of acceptance given to certain persons and social groups, and is typically used to measure conflict which exists between persons or groups. (For discussion and application of social distance used in this sense see Goode and Hatt, 1952: 26, 245-249.) Public distance (Hall, 1966: 116-120) is generally used to address an informal group at the close phase (12 to 25 feet), and the far phase, ranging from more than 25 feet, is used when addressing a formal gathering. This distance is also used between the public and an important official. Hall (1966: 118-119) also presents a useful matrix summarizing informal, or dynamic, space as a function of the various distances described above and sensory involvement by the distance and immediate receptors.

Proxemic Behavior on the Interpersonal Level

The quotation from Thoreau's *Walden*, cited at the beginning of the introductory chapter, shows insight into proxemic behavior. Hall (1964: 41-42, 1966: 89) points out that Thoreau was aware of the importance of distance, voice loudness, olfactory and thermal factors in interpersonal communication. Hall (1955, 1959, 1960, 1961, 1963a, 1963b, 1964, 1966) has frequently described the misinterpretations which often take place in cross-cultural interactions due to the differences in the structuring of space. From interviews with people involved in such interactions he isolated eight factors which provide spatial cues by asking the questions "By what means other than visual do people make spatial distinctions? How do they maintain such uniform distances from each other?" (Hall, 1963b: 1005). The factors he found to be important will be discussed below.

Postural-Sex Identifiers

Humans, being of the same species, have the same anatomical base, but such acts as walking, standing, and sitting are modified in different ways by culture. People from different cultures perform these acts differently, as LaBarre (1956: 557-559) points out. Belo (1956: 158) gives examples of Balinese posture and walking, and Hewes (1955) has described almost 100 postural variations from around the world. Hediger (1961: 37-38) makes special mention of the fact that primates are the only animals which can perform the act of true sitting, and that man does most of his thinking sitting down. Winick and Holt (1961: 173) point out the importance of the seated position by citing as examples the approach to a judge's bench, a speaker addressing the chair, and the Pope speaking *ex cathedra* from St. Peter's chair. Although there are many postural variations, Hall (1963b: 1007-1008) uses this category to indicate the sex of the interactants and whether they are standing, sitting or squatting, or prone. This variable was not used in the present research because all subjects were males, and all sat in the chairs provided.

Sociofugal-Sociopetal Axis

As was mentioned earlier, Osmond (1957) coined the useful terms sociofugal and sociopetal to refer to spatial arrangements which brought people together or kept them apart. Winick and Holt (1961) found that the ways in which group therapy members positioned themselves were forms of non-verbal communication. King Arthur communicated equality by seating his knights about a round table (Winick and Holt, 1961: 173). Sommer (1959) found that in the cafeteria of a mental hospital (which was utilized by employees and patients alike) conversations were more likely to occur between persons who sat across the corner of the table. He then asked groups of subjects to go to a table and discuss a topic and found that employees, student nurses, and non-schizophrenics sat across the corner from each other most frequently, while schizophrenics sat at distant positions and opposite each other most often. Then he placed a confederate at a table and had subjects go in individually and discuss a topic. Schizophrenics sat alongside the decoy far more often than normals and made almost no use of the corner chair. Studies have been made, primarily by small-group sociologists and social psychologists, to determine the effect of seating position on leadership in a group. Sommer (1961) used employees of a mental hospital as subjects and had each group choose a leader. The leader most often chose the end positions at the table and other members of the group sat close by. When the leader did not occupy the end position others sat opposite rather than alongside. In groups without a leader, sitting around one end of the table was preferred. He then tried to show that "people will sit across from one another UNTIL THE DISTANCE BETWEEN THEM EXCEEDS THE LIMIT OF COMFORTABLE CONVERSATION" (Sommer, 1961: 106). Pairs of subjects were asked to sit on sofas placed at varying distances from each other. When the distance was three feet or less people sat opposite each other but when the distance was greater than three feet they sat side-by-side on the same sofa. In a later study Sommer (1962: 115) concluded that "people prefer to sit across from one another rather than side-by-side. We have now learned two exceptions to this — when the distance is too far for comfortable conversation, and secondly, when the distance across exceeds the distance side-by-side." Howells and Becker (1962) found that in arranging two seats across the table from three seats, a greater number of leaders than would be expected by chance emerged from the two seat side. Leavitt (1951) maintains that centrality in a small group communication network is important. Steinzor (1950) confirms the hypothesis that in a small group seated in a circle, the greater the distance between two people the more likely they are to follow one another verbally, and concludes that location in a seating arrangement plays an important role in group interaction. Hare and Bales (1963) found this to be true in a task oriented small group experiment, but in a 'social' session group members tended to talk more to people seated next to them than other members of the group. They also found that personality variables are important, as more dominant subjects tended to choose central seats and do the most talking. Hearn (1957) found that in a small group with a leader who sat by passively, members tended to interact with people opposite them and in their line of vision rather than those next to them, but when the leader was very active in criticism and coaching just the opposite effect was observed. Bass and Klubeck (1952) concluded that in an inverted 'V' seating arrangement the seat a person chose made little difference in determining leadership. Kolaja (1954) maintains that the spatial pattern of a semi-formal small group is less important than its social pattern, and as the formality of the group increased, so did the group-orientation in the speeches of its members. Hall (1963b: 1009) mentions that "which components of the sociofugal-sociopetal axis are favored and for what transactions, is largely culturally determined. These components are also linked with the social setting and the age, status, and sex of the two parties." Hall (1966: 150) describes the inability of an Arab friend to have a conversation with him while walking along shoulder to shoulder, facing forward, which is very common for Americans. Experimental evidence suggests that Arab men do indeed face each other more directly than Americans during an interaction (Watson and Graves, 1966:978-980).

Kinesthetic Factors

Distance is, of course, an important spacing mechanism. Mention has already been made of Hall's classifications of interaction distances in humans. This category is called 'kinesthetic factors' by Hall (1963b: 1009) because it is distance determined by the potential of interactants to "strike, hold, caress, or groom" one another. Hall (1955, 1959, 1960, 1961, 1963a, 1963b, 1964b, 1966, and White, 1960) has noted in many publications the differences in cultural attitudes towards the proper distance in a given situation. He reports, for example, that an American colleague still felt uncomfortable when talking to a Frenchman after 12 years of working with the French, even though he knew that cultural attitudes were involved. Arab men in a conversation sit closer to each other than do American men (Watson and Graves, 1966: 980). In developing a technique for investigating social schemata Kuethe (1962a) noted that a high commonality existed in placing cutout figures of a child closer to a woman and a dog closer to a man, and a tendency to group human figures to a greater extent than non-human ones. Kuethe (1962b) also found that the tendency to place a man figure and a woman figure together was greater than to place two woman figures together, and man figures facing each other were placed closer than those facing away from each other. In a later experiment Kuethe (1964) observed that the subjects who reconstructed man and woman figures closer together than they were originally placed were significantly more likely to give "man" and "woman" as reciprocal responses in a word association test. Then, in a test of homosexual and non-homosexual prison inmates, Kuethe and Weingartner (1964) found that the homosexuals often failed to make man-woman figure pairings, and non-homosexuals usually would not allow man-woman figures to be separated. In replacing the figures the homosexuals placed man-man pairs too close together, while the non-homosexuals replaced the man-woman pairs too close together. Little (1965) had subjects replace figures on a grid after supplying information about the degree of acquaintance and the setting, and found that the figures were placed closer together the closer the degree of acquaintance, and the distance decreased progressively in interactions involving the office, home, and street corner. Little also had subjects place live 'actresses' after describing degree of acquaintance and setting, with similar results as in the experiment with the figures. He concluded that interaction distances are strongly influenced by degree of acquaintance and the setting in which the dyad interacts. Felipe (1966) observed that cooperating individuals sit significantly closer to each other than those who are competing or coacting, and concludes that spacing is one variable, along with eye contact, topic, and amount of smiling, which is important in small group interactions. And Feshbach and Feshbach (1963: 499) report parenthetically, in a study of fear in children, that telling ghost stories to a group of boys and girls decreased the circle in which they were sitting from 11 to three feet.

Touching

The amount and kind of touching which occurs between people is culturally defined (Frank, 1957, in Smith, 1966: 207, 1960: 10; Hall, 1963b: 1011, 1966: 147). Just as Hediger divided animal species into contact and non-contact species, Hall (1963b: 1005) places humans into these two categories. Americans and Northern Europeans typify the non-contact group, due to the small amount of touching which takes place during an interaction. Arabs, on the other hand, normally use quite a bit of contact in talking to each other. Men holding hands is a somewhat common sight in the Near East, for instance. There is empirical validation of these Arab-American differences (Watson and Graves, 1966). Winick and Holt (1961: 176) comment that in group therapy sessions some patients prefer not to sit on a sofa because they dislike being touched by others. In some cultures touching a certain part of the body is strictly forbidden. Adolf Bastian, an early ethnographer, touched a Siamese noble's head in demonstrating an anatomical point and was met with reprimands, "for in Siam there is no greater affront than to touch a superior's head" (Lowie, 1938: 35).

Eye Contact

Kortland (1962: 131), observing chimpanzees, noted that when one of the animals saw his eyes, it would stand about ten feet away, "staring thoughtfully into my eyes and scratching his arms and chest before he wandered off". Schaller (1965: 127) noted that Highland gorillas became uneasy under his constant stare, which necessitated his having to avert his eyes from time to time. He maintains that he was able to see changes of emotion in the expressive eyes of the gorillas (1965: 133-134), and further reports that gorillas made much use of their eyes in courtship (1965: 179).

The proverb "the eyes are the mirrors of the soul" reflects the importance with which humans regard the eyes as a gauge of emotion. President Johnson recently said, concerning his conference with Soviet Premier Kosygin: "It is good to sit down and look a man in the eye and try to reason with him and to have him reason with you" (Associated Press, 1967a: 6). The Roman poet Ovid, writing around the beginning of the Christian era in one of the earliest "how to do it" books in the Western world advises young men to use their eyes in communicating with their lovers: "There is a lot you can say, speaking with gesture and eye" (1960: 120), and "Let your eyes gaze into hers, let the gazing be a confession: often the silent glance brings more conviction than words" (1960: 123). The Tuareg of North Africa use eye contact a great deal, as the robes and veils of the men cover almost all of their bodies, with hands, feet and the area of the eyes being the only parts readily open to view. Murphy (1964: 1265) notes that "the Tuareg is not a mouth watcher, but rather an eye-watcher and that during interaction his eyes are fixed by the steady stare of his respondent. On one occasion, I countered this by wearing dark glasses, but my Taureg friends retaliated by the same technique and succeeded in totally effacing themselves." Hall (1963b: 1012) mentions some cross-cultural differences in eye contact. Navahos, for instance, are taught not to gaze directly at another person during a conversation, a fact evident to anyone who has ever spent any amount of time with them. The Greeks use their eyes much more than Americans, who interpret this behavior as 'staring'. Hall's (1963b: 1005) American interviewers reported an uncomfortable feeling resulting from 'the penetrating stare' of an Arab's eyes. The Arabs, on the other hand, felt that an American's indirect gaze denoted a lack of interest. Observations of Arab and American subjects indeed indicate that Arabs use eye contact more than Americans (Watson and Graves, 1966: 982). Argyle and Dean (1965) assert that of the many functions of eye contact in dyadic interaction one of the most important is the feedback provided by the gathering of information on the other person's reactions. They suggest that a person moves toward a certain distance of equilibrium with another person and maintains a certain level of eye contact. Hypotheses stating that the closer the interactants, the less the intensity of eye contact, were borne out. It should be mentioned that this study was concerned with the behavior of American subjects. Hutt and Ounsted (1966: 346) affirm the belief that eye contact is important in interaction, and report on the absence of eye contact as "a persistent and characteristic feature in children with the syndrome of 'early infantile autism'" (1966: 346). Autistic children, in a number of experiments, were found to constantly avert the gazes of others. Adults normally avoid the gaze of others only when in a state of high arousal (e.g., fear or embarrassment) (1966: 355). Chance (1962: 84) feels that gaze aversion serves as an act which temporarily cuts off sensory receptors from a potential conflict-provoking situation and minimizes arousal. A 'go-go' dancer in Wisconsin recently pointed out the importance of eye contact succinctly, if ingenuously, by commenting on the nightclub in which she worked: "I hate it when it's not crowded here. You get no response. It's nice when you get up there and they smile. Eye contact is really nice" (Associated Press, 1967b: 6).

Thermal Factors

Not much is known about the importance of heat in structuring space (Hall, 1963b: 1014). The detection of body heat no doubt plays a role in communicating embarrassment (along with visual cues) or sexual arousal. This variable was dispensed with in the present study, however, first of all because the effective measurement of heat radiation and conduction would require attachment of thermal detection devices to subjects, thus defeating the purpose of making this research as unobtrusive as possible. Secondly, questioning subjects as to whether or not they detected heat from the other person proved to be fruitless (Watson and Graves, 1966: 975). An indication that non-contact groups avoid thermal cues was quoted from an English book of etiquette: "When a Gentleman offers a Lady his chair he should engage her in conversation for a few moments, thus giving the seat time to cool" (Playboy, 1967: 23).

Olfaction

The olfaction category was also dropped from this study, due to subjects being unable to say whether or not they detected odors from the other person (Watson and Graves, 1966: 975). This might have been due to the technique of questioning subjects in each other's presence. A person detecting an odor considered bad in the framework of the subject's culture would probably try not to embarrass the other person by telling the truth. Separate questioning of subjects might provide some answers. Olfactory and thermal factors are functions of the immediate receptors, so if the cultural framework were known in regard to these factors, they could be inferred from the distance between subjects. There is little doubt that olfaction plays an important role in interactions. One only has to look at television commercials which link using the proper mouth wash or deodorant to success in business, love, family relations, and friendship. It would appear that Ovid's advice given almost 2000 years ago still applies: "See that your teeth are clean, brush them at least twice a day..., Let your breath be sweet, and your body free from rank odors...... (1960: 121).

Voice Loudness

"The loudness of the voice is modified to conform to culturally prescribed norms for (a) distance, (b) relationship between the parties involved, and (c) the situation or subject being discussed" (Hall, 1963b: 1016). The level of the American voice is 'suspiciously' low to an Arab, and Arabs seem 'loud-mouthed' to Americans (Hall, 1963b: 1005). Observations of Arabs and Americans confirmed that Arabs did maintain a higher voice level in conversations (Watson and Graves, 1966: 982).

Voice loudness is one way to maintain spacing between people. It varies from culture to culture, as pointed out by Hall (1966: 133-134). American children are constantly being told to lower their voices by their parents, but little systematic research has been done cross-culturally to discover the learning and importance of maintaining the proper voice level. Castiglione, writing in 1516, felt that an important part of the courtier's grace was "... a good voice, not too thin or soft as a woman's, nor yet so stern or rough as to have a boorish quality, but sonorous, clear, gentle, and well constituted..." (1959: 54-55). Making a good vocal impression is probably as important now as it was then.

SUMMARY

This chapter has demonstrated the importance of the structuring of space in animals, and evidence has been presented which suggests that it is equally important in humans.

Literature has been reviewed which deals with territoriality, overcrowding, and distance regulation in animals and in man; how man perceives and structures space, and how culture modifies the structuring of space.

In the final section of this chapter, the categories of proxemic behavior on the interpersonal level have been discussed, and it is with these categories that the research reported herein is concerned.

III

METHODOLOGY

This research was conducted as both an exploratory study and a descriptive study. It is exploratory, on the one hand, as not much is known about the learning of proxemic behavior, or the violation of proxemic norms, or if the eight variables isolated by Hall and discussed in the last chapter are the only important ones operable. This part of the research sought to gain insight into and familiarity with proxemic behavior on the interpersonal level. On the other hand, it is descriptive in that a wide range of proxemic behavior was measured, using Hall's (1963b) system of notation, and the influence of various factors on proxemic behavior was investigated. Finally, Hall's (1963b: 1023, 1964: 44-45) suggestion that humans can be divided into 'contact' and 'non-contact' groups was tested. Although this is not testing a theory-derived hypothesis, it takes, methodologically speaking, the same form.

RESEARCH DESIGN

The research was conducted during the spring and fall of 1966, and the spring of 1967. The sample consisted of 110 male foreign students, from various parts of the world, who were studying at the University of Colorado. Appointments with subjects were made by a foreign student who served as my assistant. He recruited subjects from among his personal acquaintances, from meetings of foreign student organizations, and from contacting potential subjects at their homes, using a list of foreign students supplied by the Office of Special Services at the University. In the spring of 1967, when data collection was scheduled to be drawing to a close, letters were sent to male foreign students who had not yet participated in the research. This method proved to be surprisingly effective, especially when the letters were followed up by a call from my assistant. My assistant knew very little about the research and was instructed to tell subjects only that their participation would take about an hour, that no tests would be administered, and that I was an anthro-

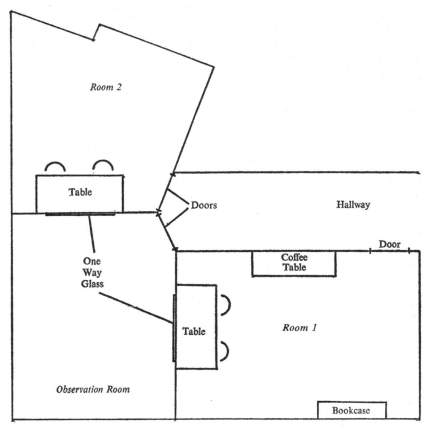

Figure 1.
Observation Rooms Scale: $1'' = 3'$

pologist who was interested in the behavior of people from different parts of the world. I later asked my assistant to assure the subjects that I was NOT a psychologist, as many subjects displayed an apprehension about being 'tricked' and I found it necessary to confirm to them that I was indeed an anthropologist in order to gain greater rapport with them.

Unfortunately, the times of observation could not be controlled, but the majority were carried out in the morning and all of them during the daylight hours. Male foreign students who were from the same country and who spoke the same native language reported to me in pairs[1] at an appointed time. They were shown into room 1 (see Figure 1) and asked

[1] Both persons in an interacting pair always receive the same score on the axis variable, and almost always on the kinesthetic (closeness) variable — the exceptions being when one subject is leaning back with the upper portion of his body and thus

to complete a short questionnaire giving basic demographic data (Appendix A). They were asked to wait for me to come get them after completing the questionnaires. Room 1 was disguised as a lounge, with paintings hung around the room, a bookcase, magazines strewn around, and a coffee pot. The one-way mirror was covered with a painting on fabric, which rendered it inconspicuous to the subjects, yet allowed observation of them. Subjects were then observed with the intention of comparing their proxemic behavior in room 1, where they were unaware they were being observed, to their proxemic behavior in room 2, where they were told of the observations being made. It took only a few subjects to demonstrate that this arrangement was a total failure. The principal difficulty was the anticipatory attitude of subjects in room 1. After completing their questionnaires, many subjects sat and waited for my return. Others looked around the room, searching for a hidden microphone, which was there, but was not discovered. One pair kept quiet, writing notes to each other and holding their hands over their mouths to keep from laughing, apparently in an effort to confound anyone listening in. It is perhaps significant that no subject discovered the one-way mirror hidden behind the painting. Observations in room 1 provided me with a source of hilarity, but no meaningful data, so this procedure was dropped and room 2 was used exclusively. After completing the questionnaires, subjects were told that I would be observing them from behind a one-way mirror, which was plainly visible, and to talk about anything, in their native language, which, I told them, I did not speak (true in the large majority of cases). Subjects were told simply that I was interested in how people from different countries acted when they talked to each other. Under certain circumstances this procedure might be considered obtrusive (Webb *et al.*, 1966). It would probably cause the subjects to react by being on their 'best behavior', and they probably were. This would be a hinderance were it not that proxemic behavior is maintained largely 'out of awareness', and thus the conscious manipulation of proxemic behavior

---

having his potential for touching his partner with his hands reduced. In an earlier study (Watson and Graves, 1966) four subjects were used to form Arab and American subgroups. Each person in a sub-group was alternately paired with the other three members of the sub-group until all the possible combinations of pairing were exhausted. Each person thereby comes to share a portion of his variance on the axis and kinesthetic measures with all the other members of the sub-group. In order to reduce this source of variance, which might be reflected in greater homogeneity within a country on these two measures, a subject from a particular country was allowed to interact with only one other person from that country, i.e., mutually exclusive pairs were used.

by the subject is mostly eliminated (Hall, 1963b: 1003). Subjects were given a few minutes to 'warm up', and then their proxemic behavior was observed and recorded over a period of five minutes. Subjects were then interviewed from 20 to 80 minutes.

DATA COLLECTION

Questionnaire (Appendix A)

Subjects were asked to complete a questionnaire giving name, age, nationality, and native language. They were also asked what other languages were spoken, understood, and read. As mentioned above, Hall thinks that proxemic behavior is maintained largely out of an individual's awareness. This makes it roughly comparable to linguistic 'style', i.e., the stress, pitch, and loudness of the voice used in a certain situation. (See Joos, 1962 for a discussion of English style.) A person knows what style to use on a certain occasion, but would probably be unable to give rules which determine the style (Hall, 1963b: 1018). This makes it particularly difficult to measure sources of change in proxemic behavior. Hall (1967) believes that in contact groups immigrating to this country, it takes at least three generations for a change to the American non-contact style to take place. Does someone have to be completely acculturated in order for his patterns of proxemic behavior to be changed? The answers to this, and many other questions which could be raised in regard to change, will have to wait until more is known about proxemic behavior. In a crude attempt to detect any change in proxemic behavior, subjects were asked how many months they had lived in an urban environment, the length of time they had spent outside their own countries, and the length of time they had spent in Europe and the United States. These seemed the most obvious sources of change which would apply to the present sample. A city is, of course, a major influence in culture change. An urban area is the recipient of ideas from all over the world, and people living in a city are constantly exposed to these sources of change. Exposure to the habits of other people, roughly measured by the amount of travel a subject had undertaken outside his country, seemed to be another obvious source of change. Finally, a subject was asked how well he knew the other member of the pair. This was to see if any differences in proxemic behavior would be encountered due to degree of acquaintance.

OBSERVATIONS

The conditions in room 2 (Figure 1), where subjects were observed, were
as neutral as possible. Noise level and temperature were controlled, and
the room was bare except for a table, at which the subjects sat in the two
chairs provided, and an extra chair at the back of the room, which was
later used by me during the interview. After the questionnaires were
completed, the subjects were told to talk about anything they wanted to,
and in their native language. The fact that they were being observed
seemed not to bother them. In fact I routinely asked the subjects, after
the observations, if the one-way mirror had bothered them. Most said
that it did not, and many said that they forgot about it as their conversations with their partners progressed. Postural-sex identifiers, thermal
factors, and olfaction were not measured, as was previously explained.
The five remaining variables, measured by a system of notation based on
Hall's (1963b), were operationally defined as follows:

Sociofugal-Sociopetal (SF-SP) Axis

This measure was based on the relation of the axis of one person's
shoulders to that of the other. These relationships were scored on a scale
of 1 through 9, as shown in Figure 2.[2]

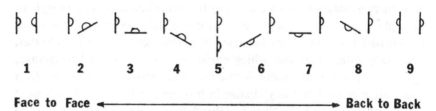

Figure 2.
Sociofugal-Sociopetal Axis

[2] The scale does not include a measure for front-to-back axis, i.e., one person facing
the back of another. The laboratory setting precluded the necessity for its use, but
examples of this axis position can be seen every day when Americans line up to buy
tickets, wait for a bus, etc. My service in the U.S. Marine Corps supplies me with an
example of an interaction in this position which has probably been experienced by
anyone serving in the military. While in ranks, as marching for instance, a person can
manage to talk to the person in front of him without being detected by his superiors
but the person to whom this attention is directed is restricted from talking to the person
behind him. This fact, for Marines at least, is a constant source of amusement. Men
in ranks are constantly harrassed by the men behind them. The men in the last rank
are fortunate not to have anyone behind them, and are thus spared from pestering.
The men in the front rank, however, have no one upon whom to transfer the abuse
which bombards them from behind.

Kinesthetic Factors

This category measures the closeness of one person to another, in terms of the potential to hold, grasp, or touch. As an aid to scoring, the edge of the table nearest the subjects was inconspicuously marked every six inches with a pencil. The pairs were scored on the following bases:

1. Within body contact distance
2. Just outside this distance
3. Within touching distance with forearm extended
4. Just outside this distance
5. Within touching distance with arm extended
6. Just outside this distance
7. Within touching distance by reaching
8. Just outside this distance
9. No potential for touch

Touch Code

This category provides for the amount and kind of contact during an interaction. It was scored as follows:

1. Holding and caressing
2. Feeling and caressing
3. Prolonged holding
4. Holding
5. Spot touching
6. Accidental touching
7. No contact

Visual Code

The coding in this category provides an index of the amount of visual contact present. The code is:

1. Sharp (focusing directly on the other person's eyes)
2. Clear (focusing about the other person's head and face)
3. Peripheral (having the other person within the field of vision, but not focusing on his head or face)
4. No visual contact (looking down or gazing into space)

Voice Loudness Scale

The level of a person's voice during an interaction is the measure provided by this category. The microphone of a tape recorder equipped with a decimeter was attached to the speaker over which the subjects' voices were heard. The subjects' voices were picked up by a microphone inconspicuously placed in the ceiling of room 2. The decimeter was divided into ranges, which provided the scoring for this category:[3]

1. Very loud
2. Loud
3. Normal plus
4. Normal
5. Soft
6. Very soft

After subjects had been talking to each other for a few minutes, observations were begun by observing and recording, each variable in turn, a line of proxemic behavior of the subject on the observer's left. The same thing was then done for the subject on the observer's right. A new line of notation, starting with the subject on the left, was begun every ten seconds.[4] The observation lasted five minutes, giving each subject a total of 30 lines of notation. During the first observations a small adding machine was used, but it turned out to be no more efficient than recording with pen and paper. For one thing, the machines were so noisy that it was suspected that subjects could hear them. Also, when a mistake was suspected, it was almost impossible to read the numbers on the adding machine tape in the darkened observation room. So the reliable pen and paper method was used in the great majority of the observations. Another observer[5] was utilized during a few of the observations, and interobserver reliability was virtually 100%. Each of the categories has fairly mechanical measures, so bias does not seem to be a problem. Subjects were not scored when they were silent, as voice loudness was to be measured, not garrulity.

[3] The accuracy of the decimeter used to measure voice loudness was not known, so ranges were marked off on it to correspond to the various voice levels described. Several friends, all Americans, held conversations in various levels of voice loudness until agreement was reached regarding the range of each level. The descriptive categories of voice loudness, e.g., 'normal', 'loud', etc., are scaled in terms of American norms. No difficulty was foreseen in useing this type of measurement. In the field, for example, the observer would use his ear in measuring relative voice loudness, and "no standards have been established for judging voice loudness EXCEPT those people learn and against which they judge the behavior of others" (Hall, 1963b: 1017).

[4] In earlier research (Watson and Graves, 1966) a line of notation was recorded every minute. With a little practice an observer can easily take a line of notation for each subject within ten seconds.

[5] I am grateful to Bryan P. Michener, who observed some interactions with me in order to establish interobserver reliability.

INTERVIEWS (APPENDIX B)

Pike (1966) has emphasized the importance of the distinction between the 'etic' and 'emic' levels of analysis. "The etic viewpoint studies behavior as from outside of a particular system, and is an essential initial approach to an alien system. The emic standpoint results from studying behavior as from inside the system" (Pike, 1966: 152). The etic level is concerned with systems of behavior shared by all humans, while the emic level takes into account the way these systems are arranged in different cultures. Pike (1966) coined these suffixes from the words 'phonetic' and 'phonemic'. Phonetics is the study of human language, the sounds which all humans are capable of making. Phonemics is the study of how a particular language uses a narrow range of possible sounds. Another frequently used illustration of the etic and emic levels of analysis applies to kinship. At the etic level, anthropologists know that all people have kinship systems, i.e., the relationship of one person to other persons in a group. But emic analysis attempts to study the ways in which the kinship system of a particular group is ordered by determining the values attached to a certain position in the system, or attitudes toward a particular relative. Proxemic behavior, presumably like all systems of behavior, can be approached in terms of etic and emic analysis. Hall (1963b), as mentioned before, has isolated several variables which seem to make up a system whereby people structure space at the interpersonal level. Hall (1963b: 1021) writes, in discussing his system of notation for proxemic behavior: "... it will be apparent to the reader that this presentation is concerned more with proxetics than proxemics, and is therefore only the first of a series of steps in a long complex process." Hall has found categories which appear to be universal, proxetics really, but little is known about the importance attached to these categories by people of different cultures, which is properly called proxemics. Barker and Barker (1961), for example, found that it was much more satisfactory to let the English subjects whom they were studying supply their own behavioral frames of reference, rather than having predetermined frames imposed on the data. One of the purposes of the interview with foreign students was to try and determine if Hall's proxemic categories were the only ones operable and whether or not some of them were superfluous.

Another purpose of the interviews was to try to pinpoint any interferences, or misinterpretations, subjects might have encountered in American proxemic behavior, and what these interferences would mean in the context of the subject's own culture. A person in a more or less alien culture, like foreign students in the United States, are not likely to understand all of the vast and subtle array of cues which are operable in an interaction. When persons from different cultures interact there is likely to be "interference between two patterns, or a perceived absence of patterning, during an encounter" (Hall, 1963b: 1005). The mention of interference by a subject would give an indication of what proxemic norms are operable in his culture, and questioning the subject further about violation of norms in his own culture would point out the values attached to these norms. Foreign students are ideal informants in regard to proxemic interferences, as they are constantly exposed to these interferences.

During the interviews an attempt was also made to find if there were any specific and explicit rules about proxemic behavior in different cultures, and how these rules were learned.

After observations were completed I went into the room and told subjects that I was interested in the ways in which people from different countries behave when talking to each other. The interview was then begun. The interview was open and fairly loosely structured, the subjects being allowed to respond freely to the questions outlined in Appendix B. All interviews were tape recorded. Subjects were asked to limit their responses to behavior between males.[6] Questions 1 and 2 (Appendix B) were attempts to get the subjects to supply categories of their own in reference to proxemic behavior. Most subjects at first made references to linguistic categories, i.e., not being able, at first, to understand English idioms, etc. When I got the idea across to them that I was interested in non-verbal behavior, they responded quite readily. Question 3 tried to uncover what interferences subjects perceived, and questions 4 and 5 were attempts to get at meanings of these interferences in the subjects' own countries. In question 6 each category of proxemic behavior which was observed, plus postural factors, were mentioned to the subjects in order to see what differences subjects had observed between Americans and themselves. Question 7 queried students as to any interferences which might have existed and the meaning of these interferences. Question 8 attempted to get subjects to talk about what rules for proxemic behavior might be operable in their cultures and the ways in which these rules

---

[6] Responses to the interview questions were limited to the proxemic behavior of males, since observations were limited to males. Not enough is known about proxemic behavior to introduce problems which would clearly arise from using male-female interactions. I was not, however, opposed to the idea of observing female-female interactions, but the female foreign student population at the University of Colorado was rather limited.

were learned. In question 9 subjects talked about regional variations of proxemic behavior in their own countries, and their impressions of the proxemic behavior of people from other countries (besides Americans) with whom they might have had contact. Upon completion of the interview subjects were paid $2.00 each for their time and were asked not to discuss the research with other foreign students who might be potential subjects.

IV

ANALYSIS OF THE DATA

Within this chapter various analytic techniques are used in describing the data obtained in this study. The sample is described, and various demographic data obtained from the questionnaires are presented. Then, data obtained from observations of proxemic behavior are reviewed. Sections dealing with the validity of the proxemic variables used in observations and the learning of proxemic behavior follow. The next section discusses the influence of acculturation and familiarity on proxemic behavior, and the final section is concerned with the relationships which exist between the proxemic variables themselves. Discussion of the data obtained concerning the meaning of proxemic behavior is presented in the next chapter.

THE SAMPLE

The sample consisted of 110 male foreign students studying at the University of Colorado who completed questionnaires, were observed and interviewed. Observations of 16 American males from an earlier study (Watson and Graves, 1966) were added to the sample for purposes of comparison.[1] The sample of foreign students represents about half the male foreign student population during any semester in the last two years. Most of the Arabs, Latin Americans, Southern Europeans, and Northern Europeans (mostly Norwegians) were obtained. Although there were a few more African males at the University than the four represented in the sample, pairs who spoke the same native languages were not available.

---

[1]   In the earlier study (Watson and Graves, 1966) a different numerical value was used to score subjects than was used in the present research. The scores of the American sample, obtained from the earlier study, were interpolated to conform to the scoring system used in the present study.

There were several more Oriental students at the University than were represented in the sample, but there were problems of contacting them. My foreign student assistants, in trying to recruit Oriental subjects, found that they do not ordinarily attend meetings and social functions of foreign student organizations. There is a Chinese Club, but it seems never to meet. Further, Oriental students generally could not be contacted at home, and very few responded to the letters sent out seeking cooperation in this project. Perhaps future research could be undertaken to find out where the Oriental students, ostensibly registered at the University, spend their time.

By far the largest gap in the sample is the representation of students from India and Pakistan. Students from these countries comprise nearly half of the foreign student population at the University, but only 12 of them were represented in the sample. This is explained largely by their unwillingness to cooperate and unreliability as subjects (from my point of view, at least). The refusal rate for India and Pakistan was high, and many students who had appointments neglected to show up, or one of a pair came and the other subject failed to appear. It should be mentioned, however, that the few Indian and Pakistani subjects who served as subjects were extremely helpful and informative.

Foreign students are not, of course, typical representatives of their countries. Compared to the large majority of their countrymen they are much more educated and more widely traveled. The subjects in this study cannot be assumed, therefore, to represent a random sample from the population of their countries. Although it is not known why students from a particular country chose the University of Colorado for their studies, or why it was chosen for them, it is probably not rash to assume that they are a representative sample of the population of foreign students studying in the United States.

DEMOGRAPHIC DATA

Countries in the sample were grouped into geographic categories for means of comparison, as will be discussed in more detail below. The Arabs were represented by subjects from Iraq, Kuwait, Saudi Arabia, Syria, and the United Arab Republic; students from China, Indonesia, Japan, the Philippines, and Thailand made up the Asian group; Indians and Pakistanis were put together into one group; Latins were represented

TABLE 1

Age of Subjects
T Test Comparison of Groups

Groups		N	Mean	S.D.
Contact	Arabs	20	24 yrs. 1 mo.	55 mos.
	Latin Americans	20	23 yrs. 8 mos.	53 mos.
	Southern Europeans	10	25 yrs. 6 mos.	32 mos.
Non-contact	Asians	12	28 yrs. 9 mos.	77 mos.
	Indians-Pakistanis	12	28 yrs. 1 mo.	72 mos.
	Northern Europeans	32	25 yrs. 1 mo.	42 mos.

		Contact		Non-contact		
		Latins	So. Eur.	Asians	Ind.-Pak.	No. Eur.
Arabs	t	.25	−1.09	−2.23	−2.05	−.85
	sig	NS	NS	p<.05	NS	NS
Latins	t		−1.37	2.41	2.24	−1.16
	sig		NS	p<.05	p<.05	NS
So. Eur.	t			1.60	1.38	−.42
	sig			NS	NS	NS
Asians	t				.23	1.90
	sig				NS	NS
Ind.-Pak.	t					1.70
	sig					NS
No. Eur.	t					
	sig					

(Contact: Arabs, Latins, So. Eur. — Non-contact: Asians, Ind.-Pak., No. Eur.)

NS = Not significant at the .05 level or better

by subjects from Bolivia, Cuba, Ecuador, El Salvador, Mexico, Paraguay, Peru, Puerto Rico, and Venezuela; the Northern Europeans group was comprised of students from Australia, England, Germany, the Netherlands, Norway, and Scotland; and finally, French, Italian, and Turkish students made up the Southern European group. These groups were further split, as will also be discussed below in more detail, into 'contact' and 'non-contact' categories. The contact group is comprised of the Arabs, Latin Americans, and Southern Europeans, while the Asians,

TABLE 2

Urban Experience of Subjects
T Test Comparison of Groups

	Groups	N	Mean	S.D.
Contact	Arabs	20	19 yrs. 7 mos.	85 mos.
	Latin Americans	20	21 yrs. 9 mos.	53 mos.
	Southern Europeans	10	19 yrs. 10 mos.	100 mos.
Non-contact	Asians	12	19 yrs. 6 mos.	145 mos.
	Indians-Pakistanis	12	16 yrs. 11 mos.	112 mos.
	Northern Europeans	32	12 yrs. 8 mos.	105 mos.

		Contact		Non-contact		
		Latins	So. Eur.	Asians	Ind.-Pak.	No. Eur.
Contact	Arabs	t	-1.26	$-.10$	.03	.80	3.00
		sig	NS	NS	NS	NS	$p<.01$
	Latins	t		.73	$-.68$	-1.70	4.90
		sig		NS	NS	NS	$p<.001$
	So. Eur.	t			$-.09$	$-.75$	-2.28
		sig			NS	NS	$p<.05$
Non-contact	Asians	t				.54	1.71
		sig				NS	NS
	Ind.-Pak.	t					1.34
		sig					NS
	No. Eur.	t					
		sig					

NS = Not significant at the .05 level or better

Indians and Pakistanis, and Northern Europeans constituted the non-contact group. Africans, due to their small sample size, were eliminated from analysis.

T tests[2] were run on the responses to questions 4 through 8 on the

[2] T tests were used because in small samples the distribution of t provides a more appropriate model than either the binomial or normal distribution (Ferguson, 1959: 126-127). The tests were two-tailed because no predictions about directions of differences between groups were made.

TABLE 3

Travel for Pleasure Outside Subjects' Native Country (in Months)
T Test Comparison of Groups

	Groups	N	Mean	S.D.
Contact	Arabs	20	6.2	5.0
	Latin Americans	20	4.3	4.1
	Southern Europeans	10	7.3	7.7
Non-contact	Asians	12	6.8	15.0
	Indians-Pakistanis	12	0.3	0.5
	Northern Europeans	32	3.4	4.3

		Contact		Non-contact		
		Latins	So. Eur.	Asians	Ind.-Pak.	No. Eur.
Arabs	t	1.3	−.41	−.12	5.31	2.10
	sig	NS	NS	NS	$p<.001$	$p<.05$
Latins	t		−1.15	.55	−4.41	.78
	sig		NS	NS	$p<.001$	NS
So. Eur.	t			−.11	−2.88	−1.54
	sig			NS	$p<.02$	NS
Asians	t				1.50	.77
	sig				NS	NS
Ind.-Pak.	t					−4.05
	sig					$p<.001$
No. Eur.	t					
	sig					

NS = Not significant at the .05 level of better

questionnaire (see Appendix A) as a way of comparing basic demographic data. Table 1 demonstrates that the Indian-Pakistani students were the oldest and the Latin Americans the youngest. The only significant differences in age were between the Arabs and Asians, the Asians and Latins, and the Indians-Pakistanis and Latins.

Table 2 summarizes the urban experience of subjects. The Latins had the most experience in cities, with a mean of 21 years and 9 months, and the Northern Europeans the least, with a mean of 12 years and 8 months.

TABLE 4

Travel for Business or Study Outside Subjects' Native Country (in Months)
T Test Comparison of Groups

	Groups	N	Mean	S.D.
Contact	Arabs	20	41.1	22.8
	Latin Americans	20	32.8	40.8
	Southern Europeans	10	27.0	39.3
Non-contact	Asians	12	37.8	27.2
	Indians-Pakistanis	12	16.7	12.6
	Northern Europeans	32	34.0	42.5

			Contact		Non-contact		
			Latins	So. Eur.	Asians	Ind.-Pak.	No. Eur.
Contact	Arabs	t	.79	1.05	.35	3.90	.77
		sig	NS	NS	NS	p<.001	NS
	Latins	t		.38	.41	−1.64	−.10
		sig		NS	NS	NS	NS
	So. Eur.	t			.73	−.80	.48
		sig			NS	NS	NS
Non-contact	Asians	t				2.44	.34
		sig				p<.05	NS
	Ind.-Pak.	t					−2.09
		sig					p<.05
	No. Eur.	t					
		sig					

NS = Not significant at the .05 level or better

Northern Europeans differed significantly from each of the contact groups.

In traveling for pleasure outside of one's native country, Table 3 indicates that the Indian-Pakistani group differed significantly from Arabs, Latins, and both Northern and Southern Europeans. The only other significant difference existed between the Arabs and Northern Europeans.

Fewer significant differences existed in traveling outside of a subject's

TABLE 5

Time Spent by Subjects in Europe (in Months)
T Test Comparison of Groups

	Groups	N	Mean	S.D.
Contact	Arabs	20	8.0	14.8
	Latin Americans	20	11.3	37.4
	Southern Europeans	10	7.1	6.0
Non-contact	Asians	12	2.1	6.3
	Indians-Pakistanis	12	0.1	0.3
	Northern Europeans	32	9.2	14.4

			Contact		Non-contact		
			Latins	So. Eur.	Asians	Ind.-Pak.	No. Eur.
Contact	Arabs	t	−.37	.22	1.55	2.37	−.30
		sig	NS	NS	NS	p<.05	NS
	Latins	t		.48	-1.07	−1.34	.23
		sig		NS	NS	NS	NS
	So. Eur.	t			−1.91	−3.71	.67
		sig			NS	p<.01	NS
Non-contact	Asians	t				1.09	−2.28
		sig				NS	p<.05
	Ind.-Pak.	t					−3.59
		sig					p<.01
	No. Eur.	t					
		sig					

NS = Not significant at the .05 level or better

native country for business or study. The Indian-Pakistani group had the lowest mean, and differed significantly from Arabs, Asians, and Northern Europeans, as seen in Table 4.

There was quite a bit of difference in the time subjects had spent in Europe, indicated in Table 5, with the Latins surprisingly spending more time in Europe than Europeans outside of their own countries. The Latins had spent an average of almost a year in Europe, while the Indians and Pakistanis spent an average of about three days.

TABLE 6

Time Spent by Subjects in the United States (in Months)
T Test Comparison of Groups

	Groups	N	Mean	S.D.
Contact	Arabs	20	35.8	13.2
	Latin Americans	20	30.1	25.9
	Southern Europeans	10	26.2	39.3
Non-contact	Asians	12	31.9	20.5
	Indians-Pakistanis	12	16.8	12.4
	Northern Europeans	32	25.0	25.8

		Contact		Non-contact		
		Latins	So. Eur.	Asians	Ind.-Pak.	No. Eur.
Arabs	t	.88	.75	.59	4.09	1.99
	sig	NS	NS	NS	p<.001	NS
Latins	t		.28	.23	−1.95	.69
	sig		NS	NS	NS	NS
So. Eur.	t			.42	−.73	−.09
	sig			NS	NS	NS
Asians	t				2.19	.93
	sig				p<.05	NS
Ind.-Pak.	t					−1.43
	sig					NS
No. Eur.	t					
	sig					

NS = Not significant at the .05 level or better

There were not as many significant differences in the time spent in the United States, as is demonstrated in Table 6. The Indians and Pakistanis had the lowest mean, and differed significantly from both the Arabs and Asians.

Table 7 points out that the Indian-Pakistani group spoke the most foreign languages, an average of 2.3, and the Arabs and Northern Europeans the least, with a mean score of 1.5. The Indians and Pakistanis differed significantly from both the Arab and Northern European groups.

ANALYSIS OF THE DATA

TABLE 7

Number of Foreign Languages Spoken by Subjects
T Test Comparison of Groups

	Groups	N	Mean	S.D.
Contact	Arabs	20	1.5	0.7
	Latin Americans	20	1.9	1.1
	Southern Europeans	10	2.0	1.1
Non-contact	Asians	12	1.9	1.1
	Indians-Pakistanis	12	2.3	1.1
	Northern Europeans	32	1.5	1.0

		Contact		Non-contact		
		Latins	So. Eur.	Asians	Ind.-Pak.	No. Eur.
Contact						
Arabs	t	−1.18	−1.36	−1.20	−2.41	0.0
	sig	NS	NS	NS	p<.05	NS
Latins	t		−.36	.17	1.21	1.11
	sig		NS	NS	NS	NS
So. Eur.	t			−.18	.73	−1.31
	sig			NS	NS	NS
Non-contact						
Asians	t				−.95	1.15
	sig				NS	NS
Ind.-Pak.	t					2.31
	sig					p<.05
No. Eur.	t					
	sig					

NS = Not significant at the .05 level or better

The only significant differences in the number of foreign languages understood was between the Indian-Pakistani and Arab groups, as Table 8 shows, with the Indians-Pakistanis again the highest (2.5) and the Arabs the lowest (1.5).

Table 9 demonstrates that the Arabs, with the lowest mean (1.6), differed significantly from the Asians, Indians-Pakistanis, Latins, and Northern Europeans in the number of foreign languages read. The

TABLE 8

Number of Foreign Languages Understood by Subjects
T Test Comparison of Groups

	Groups	N	Mean	S.D.
Contact	Arabs	20	1.5	0.7
	Latin Americans	20	2.2	1.3
	Southern Europeans	10	2.3	1.1
Non-contact	Asians	12	2.1	1.1
	Indians-Pakistanis	12	2.5	0.8
	Northern Europeans	32	1.9	1.1

		Contact		Non-contact		
		Latins	So. Eur.	Asians	Ind.-Pak.	No. Eur.
Arabs	t	−1.97	−2.17	−1.67	−3.61	−1.73
	sig	NS	NS	NS	$p<.01$	NS
Latins	t		−.34	−.16	.94	.60
	sig		NS	NS	NS	NS
So. Eur.	t			−.47	.49	−.93
	sig			NS	NS	NS
Asians	t				−1.07	.39
	sig				NS	NS
Ind.-Pak.	t					1.84
	sig					NS
No. Eur.	t					
	sig					

NS = Not significant at the .05 level or better

number of foreign languages read was generally higher than the number spoken or understood. Any Ph.D. candidate, due to the language reading requirement, can probably read more foreign languages than he can understand or speak; and as many of the subjects were graduate students, this probably explains the higher score. It is also interesting to note what a polyglot aggregation foreign students are.

TABLE 9

Number of Foreign Languages Read by Subjects
T Test Comparison of Groups

	Groups	N	Mean	S.D.
Contact	Arabs	20	1.6	0.7
	Latin Americans	20	2.3	1.1
	Southern Europeans	10	2.3	1.1
Non-contact	Asians	12	2.7	0.9
	Indians-Pakistanis	12	2.7	1.1
	Northern Europeans	32	2.3	1.1

			Contact		Non-contact		
			Latins	So. Eur.	Asians	Ind.-Pak.	No. Eur.
	Arabs	t	−2.54	−2.04	−3.74	−3.23	−3.03
		sig	p<.02	NS	p<.01	p<.01	p<.01
Contact	Latins	t		0.0	1.02	.92	.06
		sig		NS	NS	NS	NS
	So. Eur.	t			.87	.80	−.05
		sig			NS	NS	NS
	Asians	t				0.0	1.22
Non-contact		sig				NS	NS
	Ind.-Pak.	t					1.07
		sig					NS
	No. Eur.	t					
		sig					

NS = Not significant at the .05 level or better

Table 10 summarizes how well each member of a pair of subjects was acquainted. A score of one was the highest degree of friendship, and five the lowest. The Arabs were best acquainted on the average, with a mean score of 1.6, and the Latins the least acquainted, having a 3.0 mean score. There was very little variance among subjects in friendship, and the only significant difference was between Northern Europeans and Arabs.

TABLE 10

Friendship Index of Subjects
(1 = Most Acquainted, 5 = Least Acquainted)
T Test Comparison of Groups

	Groups	N	Mean	S.D.
Contact	Arabs	20	1.6	0.9
	Latin Americans	20	3.0	1.7
	Southern Europeans	10	1.8	0.5
Non-contact	Asians	12	2.2	0.7
	Indians-Pakistanis	12	1.8	0.9
	Northern Europeans	32	2.4	1.0

			Contact		Non-contact	
			Latins	So. Eur.	Asians	Ind.-Pak.	No. Eur.
Contact	Arabs	t	−2.18	−.39	−1.87	−.34	−2.80
		sig	NS	NS	NS	NS	p<.01
	Latins	t		1.93	−1.32	−1.85	.93
		sig		NS	NS	NS	NS
	So. Eur.	t			1.28	0.0	2.09
		sig			NS	NS	NS
Non-contact	Asians	t				1.11	−.87
		sig				NS	NS
	Ind.-Pak.	t					−1.80
		sig					NS
	No. Eur.	t					
		sig					

NS = Not significant at the .05 level or better

OBSERVATIONS OF PROXEMIC BEHAVIOR

Attempts at statistical comparisons country by country proved fruitless because of the small sample sizes of many countries. Countries were therefore grouped into the Arab, Asian, Indian-Pakistani, Latin American, Northern European, and Southern European categories, discussed in the previous section, on the basis of geographic proximity and shared cultural tradition. The countries were also grouped according to the responses of subjects to interview questions. Thus, Arab countries were grouped together due to common political, linguistic, religious, and social attributes, and all Arab students agreed that Arabs are very similar in their proxemic behavior, regardless of which Arab countries they came from. Latin Americans were grouped according to the same criteria, as were the rest of the countries. The only country which offered any problem was Turkey. Should Turkey be classified with the Arab countries, due to religious and social similarities, or with the Southern Europeans, due to geographic proximity? It was decided to put Turkey in the Southern European group, as most subjects, including the Turks and Arabs themselves, felt Turkey was closer to these countries proxemically than to the Arab countries.

In Chapter I it was mentioned that Hediger (1941) classified animals into 'contact' and 'non-contact' species. Similarly, Hall (1963b: 1023, 1964: 44-45) suggests that humans can be divided into the same groups. People from a contact group would interact with each other facing more directly, closer, touching more, employing more eye contact, and speaking more loudly than would members of a non-contact group. Hall (1963b: 1023) uses Arabs as an example of a contact group, and Americans as an illustration of a non-contact group. Empirical research (Watson and Graves, 1966) dealing with the proxemic behavior of Arab and American males found that Arabs conversed with each other more directly, looked each other in the eye more, touched each other more, and spoke in a louder tone of voice than did Americans in the same situation. This lends support to classifying Arabs as a contact group, and Americans as non-contact. Since this research is largely exploratory in nature, perhaps freer manipulation of the data can be allowed than would be permitted if theory-derived hypotheses were being tested. In any case, countries were then ordered according to the concept of contact/non-contact cultures, largely on the basis of subjects' responses in the interview.

Table 11 lists the contact countries and the mean score and standard deviation for each observed proxemic variable, and Table 12 for the non-contact group. As was mentioned before, country by country comparisons yielded no significant results, and Tables 11 and 12 are presented for the interested reader. All discussions which follow are in terms of geographic areas. The scores of the United States sample, as was explained above, were obtained from an earlier study.

A look at the mean scores for variable 1, axis, shows that subjects from Paraguay, Venezuela, and the United Arab Republic shared a mean score of 1.0 (Table 11), and were therefore most direct. The Australians

TABLE 11

Observations of Proxemic Behavior Means and
Standard Deviations of the Five Proxemic Variables
Contact Group (N = 50)

Groups	Countries	N	Axis		Closeness		Touch		Visual		Voice	
			Mean	S.D.	Mean	S.D.	Mean	S.D.	Mean	S.D.	Mean	S.D.
Arabs N = 20	Iraq	6	2.09	0.85	3.67	1.03	6.88	0.19	1.36	0.25	4.02	0.24
	Kuwait	2	2.05	0.03	5.81	0.03	5.06	0.00	1.23	0.32	4.17	0.01
	Saudi Arabia	3	2.99	0.95	3.12	0.19	6.61	0.59	1.17	0.16	3.82	0.43
	Syria	2	4.42	0.02	2.99	0.02	7.00	0.00	1.55	0.21	4.09	0.79
	UAR	2	1.00	0.00	3.00	0.00	6.80	0.10	1.02	0.02	4.01	0.07
Latin Americans N = 20	Bolivia	2	4.05	0.03	3.05	0.03	6.94	0.09	1.27	0.37	4.89	0.27
	Cuba	2	1.43	0.00	7.40	0.00	7.00	0.00	1.87	0.37	3.81	0.03
	Ecuador	2	3.14	0.05	3.17	0.00	7.00	0.00	1.40	0.04	4.21	0.08
	El Salvador	2	2.13	0.00	5.00	0.00	7.00	0.00	1.63	0.28	4.26	0.13
	Mexico	2	3.34	0.05	5.00	0.00	7.00	0.00	1.30	0.14	3.97	0.11
	Paraguay	2	1.00	0.00	4.87	0.00	6.49	0.02	1.33	0.28	3.85	0.08
	Peru	4	2.99	0.03	4.74	0.31	6.00	1.15	1.16	0.18	4.50	0.43
	Puerto Rico	2	2.67	0.00	6.63	0.00	7.00	0.00	1.72	0.02	3.92	0.56
	Venezuela	2	1.00	0.00	5.00	0.00	7.00	0.00	1.25	0.07	3.56	0.45
Southern Europeans N = 10	France	4	2.08	0.09	4.00	1.15	6.89	0.12	1.19	0.11	5.05	0.62
	Italy	4	1.79	0.34	5.64	0.73	6.84	0.19	1.83	0.56	4.56	0.12
	Turkey	2	3.20	0.00	2.83	0.00	6.97	0.05	1.40	0.10	3.60	0.27

TABLE 12

Observations of Proxemic Behavior Means and
Standard Deviations of the Five Proxemic Variables
Non-contact Group (N = 72)

Groups	Countries	N	Axis		Closeness		Touch		Visual		Voice	
			Mean	S.D.	Mean	S.D.	Mean	S.D.	Mean	S.D.	Mean	S.D.
Asians N=12	China	2	4.30	0.00	3.00	0.00	6.82	0.21	2.55	0.11	4.62	0.16
	Indonesia	2	3.15	0.00	5.15	0.00	7.00	0.00	1.83	0.18	4.57	0.10
	Japan	4	3.02	0.02	5.00	0.00	7.00	0.00	2.04	0.32	4.60	0.30
	Philippines	2	3.00	0.00	8.00	0.00	7.00	0.00	2.00	0.00	5.47	0.66
	Thailand	2	3.03	0.00	5.03	0.00	7.00	0.00	1.89	0.16	4.92	0.12
Indians-Pakistanis N=12	India	8	3.85	0.71	3.70	1.13	6.99	0.02	1.81	0.47	4.46	0.61
	Pakistan	4	3.09	0.10	4.43	0.49	7.00	0.00	2.52	0.37	4.25	0.58
Northern Europeans N=48	Australia	2	4.83	0.00	5.00	0.00	7.00	0.00	1.82	0.30	4.44	0.08
	England	2	3.00	0.00	8.00	0.00	7.00	0.00	1.52	0.50	4.42	0.47
	Germany	8	2.88	0.42	5.13	0.85	7.00	0.00	1.97	0.59	4.63	0.62
	Netherlands	2	4.43	0.00	3.00	0.00	7.00	0.00	1.55	0.21	4.80	0.13
	Norway	16	4.31	0.93	4.55	1.94	7.00	0.00	1.90	0.45	4.79	0.89
	Scotland	2	2.00	0.00	8.00	0.00	7.00	0.00	1.32	0.07	4.23	0.14
	USA	16	3.00	0.54	7.66	0.76	7.00	0.00	2.86	0.28	4.43	0.08

were least direct, i.e., has the highest mean score (Table 12). In general the Arabs, Latins, and Southern Europeans were somewhat more direct than were the non-contact countries.

The mean scores for variable 2 shows that Syrians interacted at the closest distance and the Filipinos and English at the farthest.

As far as touching is concerned, it can be seen from Tables 11 and 12 that many countries received a score of 7.0, i.e., did not touch at all. The subjects from Kuwait touched by far the most during the interaction. It is interesting to note that among the contact group 21 out of 50 subjects touched, while within the non-contact group only ONE Asian subject, a Chinese, and ONE Indian subject ever touched during the interaction. Note that NONE of the Northern Europeans touched during the interaction.

The mean score of the Egyptian subjects on variable 4 indicates that they employed the most eye contact during the interaction, with a mean score of 1.02, and the Americans the least, with a mean of 2.86.

Looking at variable 5, one can see that the Venezuelans had the lowest mean score (3.56), i.e., were loudest, and Filipinos the quietest with a mean of 5.47. Each country was very homogeneous on each variable, as the low standard deviations indicate. Many countries displayed no variance at all on many variables.

Tables 13 through 17 summarize the comparisons of proxemic behavior.

Looking at Table 13, which presents the data for axis, one can see that Southern Europeans display the lowest mean score, i.e., they face each other most directly during interactions, followed by the Latins and Arabs. The Asians, Indians-Pakistanis, and Northern Europeans have higher mean scores, i.e., they were less direct.

There is no overlap in mean scores between the contact and non-contact groups. Looking at the t values and levels of significance for axis, it is evident that Arabs, Latins, and Southern Europeans fall into one population on this variable, and the Asians, Indians-Pakistanis, and Northern Europeans into another. The small variation within groups can also be noted from the low standard deviations. All t tests between groups within the contact or non-contact categories failed to reach significance, whereas all comparisons across these two types WERE significant. This proxemic variable demonstrates the meaningfulness of the *a priori* grouping of countries into a contact or non-contact type.

TABLE 13

Proxemic Variable 1: Axis
(1 = Most Direct, 8 = Least Direct)
T Test Comparison of Groups

	Groups	N	Mean	S.D
Contact	Arabs	20	2.57	1.15
	Latin Americans	20	2.47	1.01
	Southern Europeans	10	2.19	0.59
Non-contact	Asians	12	3.25	0.49
	Indians-Pakistanis	12	3.59	0.68
	Northern Europeans	48	3.51	0.99

			Contact		Non-contact	
		Latins	So. Eur.	Asians	Ind.-Pak.	No. Eur.
Arabs	t	.27	1.19	−2.34	−3.18	−3.22
	sig	NS	NS	p<.05	p<.01	p<.01
Latins	t		.97	2.91	3.73	−3.87
	sig		NS	p<.01	p<.001	p<.001
So. Eur.	t			4.56	5.20	5.65
	sig			p<.001	p<.001	p<.001
Asians	t				−1.40	−1.28
	sig				NS	NS
Ind.-Pak.	t					.33
	sig					NS
No. Eur.	t					
	sig					

(*Contact* labels the rows Arabs, Latins, So. Eur.; *Non-contact* labels the rows Asians, Ind.-Pak., No. Eur.)

NS = Not significant at the .05 level or better

Table 14 concerns itself with the distances at which subjects of various groups conversed with one another during observations. The lower the score, the more closely subjects interacted. Arabs were closest and Northern Europeans the farthest. The Arabs, Indians-Pakistanis, and Southern Europeans had the lowest mean scores while the Northern Europeans, Asians, and Latins had the highest. This ordering is not in accord with the *a priori* grouping into contact and non-contact types, with Indians-Pakistanis and Latin Americans out of place.

TABLE 14

Proxemic Variable 2: Closeness
(1 = Closest, 9 = Farthest)
T Test Comparison of Groups

	Groups	N	Mean	S.D.
Contact	Arabs	20	3.53	0.99
	Latin Americans	20	4.96	1.29
	Southern Europeans	10	4.42	1.39
Non-contact	Asians	12	5.20	1.53
	Indians-Pakistanis	12	3.94	1.00
	Northern Europeans	48	5.92	1.97

			Contact		Non-contact		
			Latins	So. Eur.	Asians	Ind.-Pak.	No. Eur.
Contact	Arabs	t	−3.93	−1.82	−3.39	−1.14	−6.65
		sig	p<.001	NS	p<.01	NS	p<.001
	Latins	t		1.03	.45	−2.48	−2.38
		sig		NS	NS	p<.02	p<.02
	So. Eur.	t			1.25	−.91	2.88
		sig			NS	NS	p<.01
Non-contact	Asians	t				2.38	−1.39
		sig				p<.05	NS
	Ind.-Pak.	t					−4.88
		sig					p<.001
	No. Eur.	t					
		sig					

NS = Not significant at the .05 level or better

Table 15 indicates that none of the 48 Northern Europeans touched during an interaction. The Arabs, on the other hand, touched the most. In this variable there is again no overlap in means between the contact and non-contact types, and no significant differences between countries within a type. By contrast, five of the nine comparisons of groups across types were significant. The variances were, again, extremely low. Within the contact group, 21 of 50 subjects touched during an interaction, while only two of the 72 non-contact subjects ever touched. A comparison

TABLE 15

Proxemic Variable 3: Touch
(1 = Most Touching, 7 = No Touching)
T Test Comparison of Groups

	Groups	N	Mean	S.D.
Contact	Arabs	20	6.59	0.66
	Latin Americans	20	6.74	0.62
	Southern Europeans	10	6.88	0.14
Non-contact	Asians	12	6.97	0.09
	Indians-Pakistanis	12	6.99	0.02
	Northern Europeans	48	7.00	0.00

		Contact		Non-contact		
		Latins	So. Eur.	Asians	Ind.-Pak.	No. Eur.
Arabs	t	−.75	−1.89	−2.53	−2.74	−2.78
	sig	NS	NS	p<.02	p<.02	p<.02
Latins	t		−.96	1.62	1.83	−1.87
	sig		NS	NS	NS	NS
So. Eur.	t			1.72	2.55	2.70
	sig			NS	p<.05	p<.05
Asians	t				−.86	−1.10
	sig				NS	NS
Ind.-Pak.	t					−1.00
	sig					NS
No. Eur.	t					
	sig					

(Contact: Arabs, Latins, So. Eur.; Non-contact: Asians, Ind.-Pak., No. Eur.)

NS = Not significant at the .05 level or better

between contact and non-contact groups in regard to touching yielded a chi square value which was significant at the .001 level.

The Arabs exhibited the most eye contact during interactions, as their mean score of 1.25 in Table 16 indicates, and Northern Europeans the least. Again note the low variances and the lack of overlap between means for contact and non-contact types. The significance levels also indicate that the Arabs, Latins, and Southern Europeans constitute a population

TABLE 16

Proxemic Variable 4: Visual
(1 = Most Eye Contact, 4 = Least Eye Contact)
T Test Comparison of Groups

	Groups	N	Mean	S.D.
Contact	Arabs	20	1.25	0.23
	Latin Americans	20	1.41	0.29
	Southern Europeans	10	1.49	0.45
Non-contact	Asians	12	2.06	0.31
	Indians-Pakistanis	12	2.05	0.55
	Northern Europeans	48	2.17	0.64

		Contact		Non-contact		
		Latins	So. Eur.	Asians	Ind.-Pak.	No. Eur.
Arabs	t	−1.82	−1.55	−7.78	−4.78	−8.64
	sig	NS	NS	p<.001	p<.001	p<.001
Latins	t		−.52	5.87	3.75	−6.74
	sig		NS	p<.001	p<.01	p<.001
So. Eur.	t			3.38	2.63	4.02
	sig			p<.001	p<.02	p<.001
Asians	t				.04	−.92
	sig				NS	NS
Ind.-Pak.	t					−.68
	sig					NS
No. Eur.	t					
	sig					

(Left margin labels: Contact spans Arabs, Latins, So. Eur.; Non-contact spans Asians, Ind.-Pak., No. Eur.)

NS = Not significant at the .05 level or better

which displays more eye contact than the population made up of Asians, Indians-Pakistanis, and Northern Europeans. ALL nine comparisons between contact and non-contact groups are significant.

The level of the voice during interactions is summarized in Table 17. Low variance is again seen within each group. As in distance, the ordering into contact and non-contact types is not in accord with the empirical

ANALYSIS OF THE DATA

TABLE 17

Proxemic Variable 5: Voice
(1 = Loudest, 6 = Least Loud)
T Test Comparison of Groups

	Groups	N	Mean	S.D.
Contact	Arabs	20	3.96	0.32
	Latin Americans	20	4.14	0.46
	Southern Europeans	10	4.57	0.67
Non-contact	Asians	12	4.79	0.43
	Indians-Pakistanis	12	4.39	0.58
	Northern Europeans	48	4.32	0.81

			Contact		Non-contact		
		Latins	So. Eur.	Asians	Ind.-Pak.	No. Eur.
Arabs	t	−1.46	−2.69	−5.82	−2.36	−2.66
	sig	NS	p<.05	p<.001	p<.05	p<.01
Latins	t		−1.78	4.02	1.24	−1.15
	sig		NS	p<.001	NS	NS
So. Eur.	t			.93	−.65	−.99
	sig			NS	NS	NS
Asians	t				1.94	2.76
	sig				NS	p<.01
Ind.-Pak.	t					.32
	sig					NS
No. Eur.	t					
	sig					

NS = Not significant at the .05 level or better

data. Arabs and Latins had the lowest scores, Northern Europeans, Indians-Pakistanis, Southern Europeans, and Asians the highest.

In looking over Tables 13 through 17, a general tendency for subjects to fall into contact and non-contact groupings does appear to emerge. Table 13 shows clearly that two distinct populations appear in regard to axis. The Arabs, Latins, and Southern Europeans comprise the population which faced significantly more directly than the Asians, Indians-

Pakistanis, and Northern Europeans. The same distinct division of populations can be seen in Table 16. The Arabs, Latins, and Southern Europeans looked one another significantly more in the eye than did the Asians, Indians-Pakistanis, and Northern Europeans. Table 14, closeness, does not demonstrate these distinct differences in populations, although there are no differences between Southern Europeans and the Arab and Latin groups, and between the Asians and Northern Europeans. Perhaps the table and chairs in the observation room had something to do with injecting an exogenous variable into the situation. One could argue that the small size of the table might not have prevented subjects from conversing as closely as they liked, but might have prevented them from conversing as far away as they liked. Looking at Table 14, one can see that there are significant differences between Asians and Indians-Pakistanis, and between Northern Europeans and Indians-Pakistanis. Perhaps the Indians and Pakistanis felt it was more important to be seated at the table than to push their chairs farther apart. But this would not explain the differences between the Latin and Arab groups. From Table 14 we can see that Arabs were closer than Latins, but Table 13 shows that Latins were more direct than Arabs. If a pair were seated face-to-face, i.e., most directly, they would be prevented from getting as close to one another than they could if they were seated side-by-side, i.e., less direct. Recall that the kinesthetic (closeness) variable was scored in terms of the ability to touch or to grasp, i.e., it was scored in terms of a subject's arms. At any rate, in a more naturalistic setting perhaps even more distinct population differences would emerge.

As far as touching is concerned, in Table 15 one can see that the Arabs, Latins, and Southern Europeans do not differ significantly from each other, and neither do Asians, Indians-Pakistanis, and Northern Europeans. No Asians, except a Chinese, ever touched, and no one of the Indian-Pakistani group except one Indian touched during an interaction.

In voice loudness, Table 17, no clear dichotomy within the sample emerged, although Latins did not differ significantly from either Arabs or Southern Europeans, and the Indian-Pakistani group fell into a population with Asians and Northern Europeans.

The evidence presented above, in Tables 13 through 17, suggests that Arabs, Latins, and Southern Europeans represent a contact group, and Asians, Indians-Pakistanis, and Northern Europeans a non-contact one. Table 18 summarizes this clearly and simply. Notice that in axis, touching and visual contact there is no overlapping of means between contact and non-contact groups. In closeness, only Indians-Pakistanis overlap with

TABLE 18

*Mean Scores of Contact and Non-contact Groups
on the Five Proxemic Variables*

Contact N = 50	Axis	Closeness	Touch	Visual	Voice
Arabs N = 20	2.57	3.53	6.59	1.25	3.96
Latins N = 20	2.47	4.96	6.74	1.41	4.14
So. Eur. N = 10	2.19	4.42	6.88	1.49	4.57
Non-contact N = 72					
Asians N = 12	3.25	5.20	6.97	2.06	4.79
Ind.-Pak. N = 12	3.39	3.94	6.99	2.05	4.39
No. Eur. N = 48	3.51	5.92	7.00	2.17	4.32

the contact type, but in voice loudness both the Indian-Pakistani and Northern European group overlap with the contact type.

These non-conformations may also be due to the relatively small sample size and resulting chance variations. Further lumping of the sample helps overcome such chance factors, although it should be mentioned that it may also conceal significant non-conformities worthy of further investigation with a larger sample.

At any rate, Table 19 presents a comparison of the contact and non-contact groups. The differences between the contact and non-contact types on axis, closeness, touch, and visual contact are highly significant, with the difference on voice loudness less so.

Note that visual contact and axis yielded the highest t's, suggesting that these two variables might better be used to define the group difference than closeness and touch, i.e., direct/indirect rather than contact/non-contact, although within the non-contact groups only TWO subjects touched, within the contact groups almost half of the subjects touched. Voice loudness was the poorest indicator of anything, but this can perhaps be explained by the confines of the setting, i.e., some subjects

TABLE 19

*Comparison of Contact and Non-contact Groups
on the Five Proxemic Variables by T Test*

Groups	N	Axis Mean S.D.		Closeness Mean S.D.		Touch Mean S.D.		Visual Mean S.D.		Voice Mean S.D.	
Contact	50	2.45	0.99	4.28	1.34	6.71	0.58	1.36	0.32	4.16	0.51
Non-contact	72	3.48	0.89	5.47	1.90	6.99	0.04	2.13	0.58	4.41	0.74
t		5.9		4.1		3.5		9.4		2.3	
Df		99		122		49		116		122	
Sig		p<.001		p<.001		p<.001		p<.001		p<.05	

mentioned that voice loudness is used to span distance; or perhaps it is a function of an imprecise measuring technique.

Generally speaking, the contact/non-contact dichotomy seems meaningful at a high level of abstraction, but nonconformities suggest the possibility that there may be significant sub-types WITHIN these global types, or more than one 'dimension' of proxemic behavior along which groups can range.

There is consistent low variance so that even small samples yield large differences, and there is cultural patterning among the most sophisticated subjects within a group.

IMPRESSIONS OF AMERICAN PROXEMIC BEHAVIOR

Subjects were asked, as is indicated by question 6 in the interview (Appendix B), about their impressions of the proxemic behavior of American males, and were asked to compare it to the proxemic norms for males in their own countries. This was an attempt to see if proxemic behavior is stereotyped, as Hall (1964: 41) believes it is.

Subjects were also asked whether or not elements of American proxemic behavior bothered or offended them. This was partially an attempt to determine if any subjects might be biased toward certain American proxemic norms, and partially to determine what norms were important in a subject's proxemic patterns. If subjects were biased by some element of proxemic behavior, their impressions of Americans in regard to this element would likely be exaggerated. On the other hand, if an American proxemic norm bothered a subject, this would reflect the importance of that norm in the subject's own proxemic pattern.

Almost none of the subjects, it is interesting to note, said that they were bothered by differences in American proxemic behavior. Most of them said that they realized that there were differences in customs between the United States and their countries, and consequently were not bothered by the differences. They indicated, however, that this would be a different story among the less well educated people in their countries, who would probably feel that a violation of their proxemic norms would be 'unnatural'.

Table 20 divides the sample into the contact and non-contact groups and lists their impressions of American proxemic behavior. The "m", "s", and "l" across the upper horizontal dimension of Table 20 indicate categories into which subjects put Americans according to whether they were felt to be more, the same, or less on a particular variable than were the people of a subject's own country. The numbers in each cell indicate the percentage of subjects who rated Americans as more, the same, or less on that variable. Some subjects had no impressions concerning American differences on some variables, which explains why the total percentages do not match the total number in a sample in some cases. Subjects' impressions were then compared to the differences actually observed.

We would expect that the subjects in the contact group would find Americans, a non-contact country, to be less direct, farther, quieter, and exhibit less touching and eye contact. This seems to be the case, as Table 20 indicates. Eighty-two percent of the contact group thought Americans were less direct, 60% thought that Americans were more distant, 98% felt that Americans touched less, 60% said that Americans exhibited less eye contact, and 72% thought that they were quieter. It is interesting to note that one subject in the contact group, an Iraqi, felt that Americans touched more than Arabs. This subject told me that he personally did not like to be touched and realized that he deviated from the Arab norm concerning touching.

A look at Table 21 shows that the majority of contact subjects seem to be correct in their impressions, as the American mean scores on each variable are higher than any of the contact groups, with the exception of voice loudness, where they overlap with Southern Europeans.

TABLE 20

Impressions of American Proxemic Behavior
Contact and Non-contact Groups

	Axis			Closeness			Touch			Visual			Voice		
Contact N = 50	m	s	l	m	s	l	m	s	l	m	s	l	m	s	l
Arabs N = 20	0%	10%	90%	20%	40%	40%	5%	0%	95%	15%	25%	60%	10%	10%	80%
Latins N = 20	10%	15%	75%	0%	40%	60%	0%	0%	100%	0%	40%	60%	30%	0%	70%
So. Eur. N = 10	0%	20%	80%	0%	0%	100%	0%	0%	100%	0%	40%	60%	20%	20%	60%
Totals	4%	14%	82%	8%	32%	60%	2%	0%	98%	6%	34%	60%	20%	8%	72%
Non-contact N = 56	m	s	l	m	s	l	m	s	l	m	s	l	m	s	l
Asians N = 12	100%	0%	0%	33%	33%	33%	50%	33%	17%	84%	0%	16%	42%	16%	42%
Ind.-Pak. N = 12	0%	50%	50%	0%	50%	50%	0%	33%	67%	33%	33%	17%	17%	17%	67%
No. Eur. N = 32	22%	5%	22%	18%	73%	9%	44%	38%	18%	4%	64%	32%	84%	8%	8%
Totals	35%	41%	24%	18%	59%	23%	36%	36%	29%	30%	44%	26%	55%	14%	30%

TABLE 21

Mean Scores for the Five Proxemic Variables
Contact and Non-contact Groups vs. Americans

		Axis	Closeness	Touch	Visual	Voice
Contact Group N = 50	Arabs N = 20	2.57	3.53	6.59	1.25	3.96
	Latins N = 20	2.47	4.96	6.74	1.41	4.14
	So. Eur. N = 10	2.19	4.42	6.88	1.49	4.57
Americans	N = 16	3.00	7.66	7.00	2.86	4.43
Non-contact Group N = 56	Asians N = 12	3.25	5.20	6.97	2.06	4.79
	Ind.-Pak. N = 12	3.59	3.94	6.99	2.05	4.39
	No. Eur. N = 32	3.58	5.61	7.00	1.68	4.64

We would expect that the impressions of the non-contact group concerning American proxemic behavior would be more scattered. Since Americans themselves are members of the non-contact group, some of the non-contact subjects would be expected to say that people from their countries were the same as Americans or differed only a little, one way or the other. Unfortunately the scoring system employed does not account for small differences. Most of the non-contact subjects felt that Americans were about the same on all variables but touching and voice loudness. Thirty-six percent thought Americans touched more, and 36% thought they touched about the same, as indicated in Table 20. A look at Table 21 demonstrates that they touch the same, i.e., not at all, as the other non-contact subjects. Fifty-five percent of the non-contact subjects felt that Americans were louder, a stereotype which receives very little empirical support from this research. Another contradiction stems from the fact that over half of the non-contact subjects felt that Americans employed about the same distance in interaction, but the mean scores in Table 21 indicate that they interacted at a greater distance than any of the non-contact groups. Perhaps the high American mean score on closeness is somehow a function of the observation room.

In summary, the impressions of American proxemic behavior held by foreign students seems to be generally corroborated by empirical evidence, although the stereotype of the 'loud American' was not supported and evidence for American distance had not been observed by the foreign students.

It should be mentioned here that the subjects, when asked about the proxemic behavior of other foreigners besides Americans, had few impressions due to a lack of contact with other foreigners for any significant length of time. Responses were so few and so scattered that they are not reported here.

VALIDITY OF PROXEMIC CATEGORIES

Questions 1 and 2 of the interview (Appendix B) were attempts to get the subjects to supply categories of behavior which were important to them in interaction, hopefully proxemic categories. Almost all of the subjects responded that Americans appeared to be much more relaxed and friendly, but that this friendliness led them to become suspicious of the sincerity of Americans. Several subjects mentioned that American men seemed to treat friendship less seriously than they were accustomed to, and that American friendships had an aura of superficiality. One Japanese subject said that he was confused by the American expression "see you later". He took it to mean that the Americans who said it would go out of their way to see him, but in most cases the bewildered Japanese never saw them again. In the same vein, an Indian mentioned that an American told him to "come over and see him". The Indian did call on him and surprised the American, who was less than hospitable. A German told me that he was completely unprepared for the American greeting "how are you". He took it literally and was flattered at the interest Americans took in him, and went to great lengths explaining his general state of health. Americans grew impatient and the German wondered what went wrong.

These responses are interesting and pertinent, but yield little information as to the validity of proxemic variables. There were few unsolicited responses pertaining to categories of proxemic behavior. Several Arabs, Latins, and Southern Europeans mentioned that Americans employed less touch in their interactions, and a few said that Americans were quieter and employed less eye contact. Some Asians said that Americans touch more, and an Indian subject said that they looked in the eyes more. Most Northern Europeans said that Americans were "about the same", but that they touch less because they do not shake hands as much as Europeans in general. Two subjects from Pakistan thought that Americans

were quieter. Other than these scattered responses, no pertinent information was obtained. Hall (1963b: 1003) knew what he was talking about
when he wrote of proxemic variables: "Direct questioning will yield few
if any of the significant variables ...".

When the categories were presented to the subjects for discussion,
however, almost all of the subjects had comments on all variables. This
would indicate that the measures ARE pertinent, if perhaps not the ONLY
pertinent ones. It seems reasonable to continue using these categories
until more revealing methods demonstrate otherwise.

THE LEARNING OF PROXEMIC BEHAVIOR

In response to question 8 on the interview (Appendix B) subjects could
remember almost no rules they were taught concerning proxemic behavior. Many subjects said that their parents told them not to talk so
loudly when they were young, but it is doubtful that this has anything to
do with proxemic behavior, but rather the inability of children to control
their voices. One Chinese subject said he learned some proxemic norms
from an etiquette book, and the Southeast Asians have a rule not to
touch anyone on the head. A subject from El Salvador pointed out the
importance of eye contact in his country by saying he remembered a rule
his parents taught him which states that if you are too embarrassed to
look a person in the eye, look at his nose so as to give the impression
that you are looking in the eye. An English subject said that the English do
not like to be touched and that not touching is "bred into you". A Japanese subject said that Japanese parents teach their children to bow and look
at the chest area when greeting people.

Most of the subjects felt that they learned proxemic behavior in-
formally, to use Hall's (1959) term. That is, they learn from imitating
other people and are not given technical examples to follow, for the most
part. The explanations by subjects about how they learned proxemic norms
concurs with a widely accepted concept of learning theorists that children
learn a large part of their adult behavior by imitation (e.g. see Bandura,
1962).

THE INFLUENCE OF EXOGENOUS VARIABLES
ON PROXEMIC BEHAVIOR

In an attempt to discover what effect certain experiential variables had
on proxemic behavior, correlations (Pearson's r) were run between re-

sponses on subjects' questionnaires (Appendix A) and the five proxemic variables observed. The correlation matrix appears in Table 22.

TABLE 22

Correlation Matrix of Proxemic Variables and Experiential
(Demographic) Variables for All Countries

	1. Axis	2. Closeness	3. Touch	4. Visual	5. Voice
6. Age	−.03	.19	.08	.16	.02
	NS	p<.05	NS	NS	NS
7. Urban Experience	−.19	−.11	−.16	−.13	−.15
	NS	NS	NS	NS	NS
8. Travel for Pleasure	−.19	−.05	−.01	−.17	−.05
	NS	NS	NS	NS	NS
9. Travel for Business or Study	−.09	−.02	−.01	−.01	.01
	NS	NS	NS	NS	NS
10. Time Spent in Europe	−.14	−.04	−.02	−.11	−.09
	NS	NS	NS	NS	NS
11. Time Spent in United States	−.17	.14	.01	.06	−.03
	NS	NS	NS	NS	NS
12. Languages Spoken	−.09	−.06	−.07	.15	−.20
	NS	NS	NS	NS	p<.05
13. Languages Understood	−.01	.06	.13	.19	.02
	NS	NS	NS	NS	NS
14. Languages Read	−.02	.14	.21	.24	.05
	NS	NS	p<.05	p<.02	NS
15. Friendship Index	−.26	.54	.37	−.06	.08
	p<.05	p<.01	p<.01	NS	NS

NS = Not significant at the .05 level or better

Although the correlations of urban experience with the proxemic variables do not quite reach significance, an interesting trend emerges: urban experience correlates negatively with all proxemic variables, i.e., the LOWER the score on urban experience the HIGHER the score on proxemic behavior, and vice versa. This suggests that the less time a subject spent in a city, the less direct, farther, less likely to touch and use eye contact, and quieter he would be; and the more time he spent in a city, the more like a person from a contact group he would become.

This would be an intriguing relationship between variables, since it runs counter to our expectations, but there is another explanation available. Looking back at Table 2, which is a t test comparison of groups on urban experience, we see that significant differences exist between the

Northern Europeans and the Arab, Latin, and Southern European groups. The Northern Europeans, who scored higher on proxemic variables, spent significantly less time in cities than Arabs, Latins, or Southern Europeans, all of which groups scored lower than Northern Europeans proxemically. Herein probably lies the explanation of the negative correlations. Unfortunately, not much can be determined about the effects of urbanization on proxemic behavior from this over-all correlation.

Traveling outside one's own country for pleasure seems to have no effect on proxemic behavior, as no significant correlations were reached with the proxemic variables (Table 22). This is no surprise, for the mean scores for this factor are all quite low (Table 3).

Traveling for business or study outside the subjects' native countries also seems to have little relationship to proxemic behavior. Although the mean scores (Table 4) for this variable were considerably higher than those for the previous variable, the correlations with proxemic variables were very low.

Correlations of time spent in Europe, time spent in the United States, languages spoken, understood, and read with the proxemic variables also tell us very little about the influences of these factors on proxemic behavior. The only significant correlations reached were between languages spoken and voice loudness, and between languages read and both touching and visual contact (see Table 22).

As far as friendship is concerned, significance was reached with axis, closeness, and touch (see Table 22). Correlations indicate that the less acquainted a pair is the more direct they will be; and the more acquainted a pair of subjects, the closer they are and the more they touch.

One problem with the analysis is that a host of other variables also differentiating subjects have not been controlled. If the sample were larger these might be cancelling each other out, and therefore be of less influence.

To control for at least some of these factors, the sample was broken down into the same contact and non-contact groups as have been discussed, and correlations were run between proxemic variables and experiential variables within each type, as indicated in Tables 23 and 25.

Looking at the correlations within the contact group (Table 23), we see that there are no significant correlations between any of the proxemic variables observed and age, urban experience, travel for pleasure, travel for business or study, and time spent in Europe. The time spent in the United States is negatively correlated with voice loudness, i.e., the more time spent in the United States, the louder a foreign student from a

TABLE 23

Correlation Matrix of Proxemic Variables and

Experiential (Demographic) Variables: Contact Group

	1. Axis	2. Closeness	3. Touch	4. Visual	5. Voice
6. Age	−.21	−.09	−.02	−.05	−.15
	NS	NS	NS	NS	NS
7. Urban Experience	−.27	.14	−.09	−.07	−.09
	NS	NS	NS	NS	NS
8. Travel for Pleasure	.06	−.01	.10	.01	.06
	NS	NS	NS	NS	NS
9. Travel for Business	−.08	−.08	.03	−.01	.23
or Study	NS	NS	NS	NS	NS
10. Time Spent in	−.21	.03	−.01	−.06	−.04
Europe	NS	NS	NS	NS	NS
11. Time Spent in U.S.	.10	.05	.10	.25	−.35
	NS	NS	NS	NS	$p<.02$
12. Languages Spoken	−.28	.30	.13	.38	−.18
	$p<.05$	$p<.05$	NS	$p<.01$	NS
13. Languages	−.30	.47	.18	.41	−.07
Understood	$p<.05$	$p<.01$	NS	$p<.01$	NS
14. Languages Read	−.17	.51	.25	.38	.01
	NS	$p<.01$	NS	$p<.01$	NS
15. Friendship Index	.13	−.31	.36	−.14	−.26
	NS	$p<.05$	$p<.05$	NS	NS

NS = Not significant at the .05 level or better

contact group becomes. Time spent in the United States was intended to be a measure of acculturation to American proxemic norms, but if this were true the contact subjects would be expected to approach American norms for voice loudness, i.e., to be QUIETER, not louder. Perhaps this relationship can be explained as a function of restrictions in voice loudness a person feels in his own country, where his behavior is subject to more censure than it would be in a foreign country.

Languages spoken, understood, and read can be seen as extremely crude indices of 'cosmopolitanness', and the expectation was that they might be associated with a shift toward non-contact proxemic norms. Languages spoken correlated significantly with three of the five proxemic variables observed (see Table 23): negatively with axis, and positively with both closeness and eye contact, i.e., the more languages spoken the more direct a contact subject will be, the farther he will be, and the less eye contact he will display. Again, if this measure can be taken to be an index of 'cosmopolitanness', we would expect the contact group to move toward the American-Northern European syndrome of urbanization-industrialization and display non-contact norms. This is contradicted if the contact subjects are MORE direct the MORE languages they speak. The correlations with distance and eye contact would seem to confirm the move toward non-contact norms, however. The same tendencies are also to be found in regard to languages understood and languages read, although the correlations do not reach significance.

Looking at the correlation of the friendship index to the five proxemic variables (see Table 22), we see that friendship is negatively correlated with closeness at a significant level, and positively with touching, i.e., the better the contact subjects knew each other, the farther away from each other they interacted and the more they touched. Several contact subjects mentioned that distance was not very important in interactions with friends, and the better a person knows another, the less important distance becomes. Subjects also mentioned that the better a person knows another, the more likely he is to touch him. Perhaps these explanations are reflected in the correlations of these variables.

In order to get a clearer picture of the relationships between the proxemic variables and possible sources of influence, trend analyses were made. Each contact group was, by means of a median split, divided into a 'high' and a 'low' category on each proxemic variable and on urban experience, time spent in the United States, and number of foreign languages spoken. The contact subjects were then grouped into 2×2 tables accordingly, as Table 24 indicates. If any factors had an influence on any of the proxemic variables, one would expect a significant number of the subjects to fall into the 'high-high' or 'low-low' cells of the tables. If, say, urban experience had an influence on proxemic behavior, then the longer a contact subject spent in a city the HIGHER his proxemic scores would be, i.e., the more like a non-contact subject he would be. We see, looking at Table 24, that this is generally not the case in regard to urban experience and proxemic behavior. In the relationship of time spent in the United States there is a significant relationship with touching (with a chi square score at the .01 level). Responses to interview questions by contact students give interesting clues to this relationship. Many contact subjects, particularly Arabs, who have a habit of male hand holding, mentioned that they had not been in this country very long before they realized that to touch each other as much as they ordinarily would in their own countries would be looked upon as homosexual behavior in the United States. They then made conscious efforts not to touch other males as much as seemed normal. One Italian subject stated the

TABLE 24

Trend Analysis of the Five Proxemic Variables and
Urban Experience, Time in United States, and Languages Spoken

		Axis		Closeness		Touch		Visual		Voice	
		Hi	Lo	Hi	Lo	Hi	Lo	Hi	Lo	Hi	Lo
Urban Experience	Hi	14	14	15	13	16	12	14	14	11	17
	Lo	10	12	11	11	13	9	12	10	15	7
Time in U.S.	Hi	13	11	13	11	19	10	11	15	14	12
	Lo	11	15	13	13	5	16	13	11	10	10
Languages Spoken	Hi	6	17	15	8	13	10	13	10	10	13
	Lo	18	9	11	16	16	11	13	14	16	11

case very nicely: "When I first came here I made conscious efforts not to touch as much as I would at home. Now I unconsciously don't touch as much." One can imagine that many contact subjects will return to their native countries with a good education, but deviating from their native touching norms.

In regard to languages spoken and proxemic behavior, the significant negative correlation between axis and languages spoken (see Table 23) is reflected in the trend analysis (see Table 24), as does the significant positive correlation between closeness and languages spoken, but the relationship between eye contact and languages spoken reflected in the correlations disappears in the trend analysis.

Moving now to the correlations within the non-contact group (Table 25) one can observe that, as within the contact group, no significant correlations exist between any of the proxemic variables and age, urban experience, travel for pleasure, travel for business or study, or time spent in Europe. A negative relationship on a significant level exists between axis and time spent in the United States, i.e., the more time spent in the United States, the more direct a subject from a non-contact group becomes. Looking back at Table 21, one can see that the mean scores for axis among the non-contact subjects is higher than that for Americans. Perhaps, then, the more non-contact foreigners are exposed to the United States, the more like Americans they become in regard to directness.

There also exists among the non-contact group a puzzling negative correlation on a significant level between closeness and both languages spoken and languages understood, i.e., the more languages a non-contact

TABLE 25

Correlation Matrix of Proxemic Variables and Experiential (Demographic) Variables: Non-contact Group

	1. Axis	2. Closeness	3. Touch	4. Visual	5. Voice
6. Age	−.22	.19	.13	.02	−.05
	NS	NS	NS	NS	NS
7. Urban	.07	−.09	−.08	.17	.06
Experience	NS	NS	NS	NS	NS
8. Travel for Pleasure	−.14	.01	.07	−.14	.02
	NS	NS	NS	NS	NS
9. Travel for Business	−.02	.02	−.23	.08	.17
or Study	NS	NS	NS	NS	NS
10. Time Spent in Europe	.06	−.07	.08	−.09	−.09
	NS	NS	NS	NS	NS
11. Time Spent in	−.26	.25	−.13	.14	.26
United States	p<.05	NS	NS	NS	NS
12. Languages Spoken	.02	−.28	−.21	.10	−.25
	NS	p<.05	NS	NS	NS
13. Languages	.21	−.31	−.16	.12	−.02
Understood	NS	p<.05	NS	NS	NS
14. Languages Read	.01	−.15	−.11	.16	−.05
	NS	NS	NS	NS	NS
15. Friendship Index	−.54	.68	.27	−.37	.01
	p<.01	p<.01	NS	p<.02	NS

NS = Not significant at the .05 level or better

subject speaks and understands, the closer he will be. Since Americans have a higher mean score for distance (see Table 21), i.e., they are farther than any of the other non-contact groups, this means that the non-contact groups move farther from Americans in direct proportion to the number of languages they speak and understand. Causal inferences probably cannot be made in this case. The explanation probably is that the relationship between distance and the number of languages spoken and read was just an artifact of the attributes of the non-contact subjects.

Looking at the significant correlations between the friendship index and proxemic variables (Table 25), one sees that the better non-contact subjects knew one another, the less direct they were, the less eye contact they employed, and the closer they were. The correlations are perhaps explained by responses made by non-contact subjects during the interview. Many said that the better a person knows another, the less important directness and eye contact are, and the better a person knows another, the closer he will interact with him.

It seems that more questions on the influence of demographic variables on proxemic behavior have been raised than have been answered. The correlations seem to indicate that urbanity or cosmopolitanness have very little influence on the proxemic behavior of either the contact or non-contact groups. The urban experience measure is probably the most clear-cut of all of the other measures of urbanity, yet very low correlations are generally found between length of time spent in a city and proxemic behavior. Surely the measures of urbanity and acculturation need refinement, but it may be the case that few exogenous factors have any influence on proxemic behavior, once a particular pattern is learned.

THE PROXEMIC SYNDROME

Table 26 presents a correlation matrix of all five proxemic variables across all countries. Looking at the matrix, interesting relationships between variables can be seen. Axis is negatively correlated, at a significant level, with distance, i.e., the closer one is to another person the less directly one faces him, and vice versa.

TABLE 26

Correlation Matrix of the Five Proxemic Variables
for All Countries ($N = 126$)

	Axis	Closeness	Touch	Visual	Voice
Axis		−.30	.25	.26	.17
		$p < .01$	$p < .01$	$p < .01$	NS
Closeness			.09	.38	−.03
			NS	$p < .01$	NS
Touch				.28	.05
				$p < .01$	NS
Visual					−.11
					NS
Voice					

But axis is correlated positively with touching and visual contact. This suggests that the more direct a person is, the more touching and eye contact take place. Among the other significant correlations are a positive one between closeness and eye contact, i.e., the closer one is to a person, the more eye contact, and vice versa. The last significant correlation is a positive one between touching and eye contact. The more touching which takes place in an interaction, the more eye contact, and vice versa. An often mentioned caution (e.g. Blalock, 1960: 337-343) about inferring causal relationships from correlations is repeated here. Because eye contact and touching, for instance, are positively correlated at a significant level does not imply that a great deal of touching necessarily CAUSES a great deal of eye contact, or that when a person looks another in the eye, that CAUSES more touching in the interaction. A significant positive correlation simply means that two variables CO-VARY significantly, i.e., they 'go together'. These correlations do indicate, however, that axis, distance, touching, and visual contact are more important than voice loudness in the contact/non-contact syndrome, but perhaps this is an artifact of the laboratory setting in which observations were recorded. For example, one Australian subject said that he thought that he and his partner were behaving normally, except that the voices were not quite as loud as they would have been in a more natural situation.

An earlier study (Watson and Graves, 1966) indicated a high correlation between proxemic variables when Arabs and Americans were grouped, but these correlations disappeared or reversed themselves when run WITHIN the American and Arab groups. In an attempt to see if there is a general system of correlations between all the proxemic variables, as there appeared to be in over-all correlations in the earlier study, i.e., one element of proxemic behavior which would be a meaningful indicator of contact and non-contact categorizations; or whether there were sub-systems and multiple dimensions, correlations were run WITHIN the contact and non-contact groups. By correlating the proxemic variables within these types, more homogeneous groups of subjects and a more attenuated range on the scales are the result, thus leading to greater instability in the correlations.

Table 27 presents the correlation matrix for the contact group, and Table 28 represents the non-contact group. The same significant negative correlation between axis and distance that was seen in over-all correlations is seen in both the contact and non-contact groups. This correlation seems anomalous at first glance, but can be explained as an artifact of the chairs used in the observations. As mentioned before, if a person were talking to another person while standing, he could get as close to the other person as he wanted. If two persons were seated, and faced each other directly, the chairs would not allow them to come nearly as close as they could if they were standing. Keep in mind that the closeness referred to above is defined in terms of the potential to grasp and feel with one's hands. Within the contact group (Table 27) the only other significant correlation is a positive one between closeness and visual contact. This

TABLE 27

Correlation Matrix of the Five Proxemic Variables
Contact Group (N = 50)

	Axis	Closeness	Touch	Visual	Voice
Axis		−.38	.15	−.08	.10
		p<.02	NS	NS	NS
Closeness			−.09	.37	.13
			NS	p<.01	NS
Touch				.21	−.05
				NS	NS
Visual					−.01
					NS
Voice					

TABLE 28

Correlation Matrix of the Five Proxemic Variables
Non-contact Group (N = 72)

	Axis	Closeness	Touch	Visual	Voice
Axis		−.65	−.14	−.06	.14
		p<.01	NS	NS	NS
Closeness			.19	.20	−.23
			NS	NS	NS
Touch				−.09	−.04
				NS	NS
Visual					−.41
					p<.01
Voice					

relationship appeared at the same level of significance in the over-all correlations, but decreases within the non-contact group (Table 26). Within the non-contact group, the only significant correlation besides axis and distance is a negative one between eye contact and voice loudness. This relationship also appears in the over-all correlations and the contact group correlations, but not at a significant level. This suggests that the louder a person talks, the less eye contact he displays. No ready explanations can be given for this puzzling relationship. The interviews with subjects yield no clues. Perhaps there is universal listening behavior where a person listens to another person, looking him in the eye and responding rhetorically in a low voice. Or perhaps these two variables are used interchangeably to bridge distance. One Arab student COULD have suggested this when he said that Arabs use either eye contact or voice loudness to span a distance, but this would not necessarily explain the high negative correlation within the non-contact group; and no response similar to the one given by the Arab student was obtained from among the non-contact group.

Hall (1966: 2-3, 5) has found in his research that people from different cultures inhabit different sensory worlds much of the time, and "do not use the same senses even to establish most of the distances maintained during conversations" (1966: 3). Perhaps the fact that NO Asian student could think of what it would mean if a person in his own culture were more direct or less direct than was normal is a reflection of different 'sensory worlds'.

There is also the possibility that sub-systems within a proxemic system are operable. Perhaps eye contact and axis make up one such sub-system, for instance, which might classify people along a direct/indirect dimension. Or perhaps closeness and touch form another such sub-system, which would determine what groups were contact or non-contact.

These suggested relationships between proxemic variables are tantalizing, but confirmation must wait until a culturally specific system of proxemic behavior is fully described and explained.

V

THE COMMUNICATIVE ASPECTS OF
PROXEMIC BEHAVIOR

Although the research reported in this dissertation was not concerned with testing hypotheses or building theories, an attempt will be made in this chapter to view proxemic behavior in a theoretical framework as a form of non-verbal communication.

Toward this end, the chapter is divided into four sections, the first of which is a description of a general model, provided by Altman and Lett (1967), which classifies the ecology of interpersonal interactions. The second section deals with the meaning of proxemic behavior, using data obtained from interviews with foreign student subjects. The next section describes interferences which occur when different systems of proxemic behavior clash, and the consequent alienation from interaction. The final section views proxemic behavior in the framework of Altman and Lett's (1967) general classification model.

A GENERAL CLASSIFICATION MODEL

Language, although the primary system whereby people communicate, is not their only method. Proxemic behavior is an example of a system of NON-verbal communication. As a system of communication, Hall (1963b: 1021) sees proxemics as "... a transaction between two or more parties, or one or more parties, and the environment." Researchers in the field of environmental, or ecological, psychology also express an interest in the transactions of man and his environment. Altman and Lett (1967: 1) define the interests of this field as "the nature of the MUTUAL interaction between man and his environment...," and assert that a better understanding of human behavior can be attained by studying "how people use their bodies and manipulate objects in their environment..." (1967: 3). They further offer a classification model, limited to the use of the environment in interpersonal relationships, which serves as a useful frame-

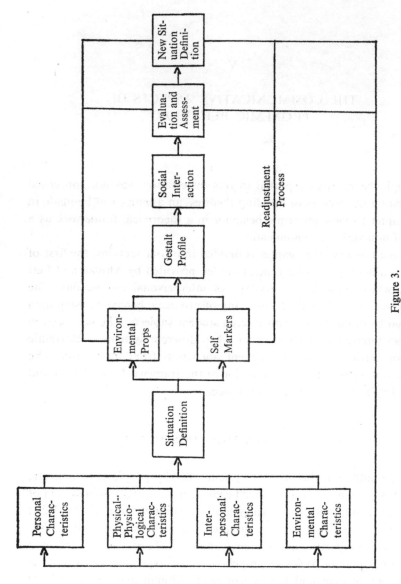

Figure 3.
A General Classification Model
(After Altman and Lett 1967)

work in which to view proxemic behavior. A simplified representation of Altman and Lett's (1967) model appears in Figure 3, and refers to dyadic interactions.

The column of elements at the far left of the model (Figure 3) are referred to by Altman and Lett (1967: 12) as "antecedent factors", and serve as means for interactants to "size up" an interaction. The "personal characteristics" category includes demographic variables such as age and sex, personality traits, and socio-cultural affiliation. The next group of antecedent factors, the "physical-physiological characteristics", refer to the "height, weight, and socially important physical characteristics..." (Altman and Lett, 1967: 14), and the physiological state of an interactant, i.e., physiological changes brought about by anger, fright, etc. "Interpersonal characteristics" refer to the degree of compatibility and friendship which exists between members of a dyad (or group). "Environmental characteristics" take into consideration "the set of events which impinge on the group from the outside" (Altman and Lett, 1967: 15), e.g., temperature of the room, amount of light, etc. These antecedent factors, as Altman and Lett (1967: 12) put it, "... serve as initial determinants of subjective expectation or SITUATION DEFINITIONS", the next step in the model. The 'situation definition' is the way in which an interactant defines the situation in which he finds himself, and he adjusts his behavior accordingly, using 'environmental props' and 'self-markers'. Environmental props refer to the ways in which people use parts of the physical environment in their interactions, tables and chairs, for instance. Self-markers are the ways in which people use their own bodies in an interaction. The next steps in the model are the 'Gestalt profile' and the 'social interaction' categories. "... The use of specific environmental props ... is integrated with the use of the 'self' (gestures, positions, vocal style) into an overall GESTALT PROFILE or behavior syndrome, which is conveyed during a temporal period of SOCIAL INTERACTION" (Altman and Lett, 1967: 13). The 'evaluation and assessment' step in the model provides a category wherein the judgments of interactants as to the appropriateness of their behavior is placed. If a person judges his behavior inappropriate in terms of the evaluations about his expectations of the situation, the model hypothesizes that he has two choices. He can either define a new situation, or, by means of feedback loops built into the model, a readjustment is made within the framework of the expectations originally defined at the initiation of the interaction. Goffman (1957, in Smith, 1966: 104) could have been describing the model when he wrote: "When individuals are in one another's immediate presence, a multitude of words, gestures, acts, and minor events become available, whether desired or not, through which one who is present can intentionally or unintentionally symbolize his character and his attitudes."

THE MEANING OF PROXEMIC BEHAVIOR

In an attempt to get at the meanings of different proxemic categories within the subjects' cultures, they were asked about differences of proxemic norms between Americans and people of their countries, and what violations of these norms meant (see questions 1 through 7, Appendix B).

Although postural variables were not measured in this research, since all subjects sat, foreign students were asked their impressions of the way Americans stood or sat when interacting. The overwhelming reply was that Americans were much more relaxed, and that they put their feet up on tables. This behavior would be condemned as impolite and disrespectful in every country represented in the sample. One Arab student said that a young Arab would put his feet up in the presence of his peers as an intentional insult, and one Norwegian said that if one of his countrymen put his feet up on the table it would be a sign of self-assurance, and the offender would probably be trying to tell everyone he had been to America. Elevating one's feet in a variety of situations seems to be a typically and exclusively American habit, judging from the responses of my informants.

Africans

Questions regarding the five proxemic variables which were observed yielded interesting answers also. Among the African group, the Kenyans said that raising the voice was impolite, and that if one saw a friend on the street in Kenya one would not shout at him, but would wait for the friend to come near before speaking. The Nigerians told me that standing too close or too far from a person when talking to him is disrespectful, and that an elder or person of higher status must not be looked directly in the eye in a conversation, as that conveys an impression of aggressiveness which is impolite.

Arabs

Among the Arabs, not facing directly enough or turning away during a conversation would indicate that one is not paying attention and would be impolite. The Arab subjects also indicated that directness is not as important as eye contact during a conversation. Although the Arabs interacted the closest of any group observed, several Arab subjects said that distance is not very important, and said that an Arab compensates for distance by shouting and eye contact. The Arabs were very aware that their custom of male hand-holding was looked upon as homosexual behavior in the United States, and made conscious efforts to avoid it. Several Arab subjects told me of their embarrassment when they were greeted by a friend, just arrived in this country, who insisted on holding hands. Although the Arabs touch more than Americans, one subject, from Iraq, said that TOO much touching in the Arab world had homosexual connotations, but, on the other hand, it is a personal preference for an Arab not to touch another Arab as much as is common. This would be looked upon as unusual, but not strange. All the Arabs emphasized the importance of eye contact in interactions. One subject said that conversation is impossible without the use of the eyes. The importance of eye contact was emphasized by one Egyptian student who had gotten into the habit of wearing sunglasses. His friends would frequently say to him, "Take off your dark glasses so I can talk to you." To an Arab, less eye contact than is considered normal is taken to mean impatience to break off a conversation, or lack of interest in the conversation. Many Arabs expressed annoyance at Americans, who employ less eye contact during a conversation. It was mentioned that an Arab raises his voice to span distance, and that loudness and distance are inversely related. Raising the voice would also mean excitement or insistence, not necessarily anger. One subject, from the U.A.R., felt that a leader should have a "loud, forceful voice". An Arab who is quieter than normal would be considered to be shy. One Iraqi, who had visited England, expressed surprise at the low voice level of the English people. "A thousand people on an English train and you can hardly hear them", he said. He was bewildered as to how a nation of such shy people could have done so well in World War II.

Asians

The Asians, like the Arabs, were very homogeneous in their descriptions of proxemic norms. The Asians frequently mentioned the importance of status in interpersonal relations. The person of higher status seems to have the prerogative to do what he wants proxemically, and the burden of correct behavior is on the person of less status. The Asians were surprisingly reticent about directness of facing, none of them being able to think of any meanings for different degrees of shoulder axis. Standing closer than normal in Asia would imply that a person thinks he is superior, as would touching a person more than is normal. Touching a person in an argument would indicate loss of self-control. More eye contact than usual would also imply superiority and would therefore be disrespectful. One Chinese subject mentioned that Americans look directly in the eye when trying to make a point, and that he was at first insulted by this. More than usual eye contact would also be looked upon as anger or threat behavior, said one Japanese student. Raising the voice seems to mean loss of control during anger among the Asian students. Violations of proxemic norms among the Asian subjects seems to imply a higher status than one perhaps has, and is thus insulting and disrespectful.

Indians-Pakistanis

Whereas the Asian group mentioned status to be an important determinant of proxemic behavior, the Indian-Pakistani group gave the same importance to the degree of friendship. They were in agreement that Indian and Pakistani friends were similar to American friends in proxemic behavior, but maybe a little closer, using a little more eye contact and a little more touching. When meeting someone for the first time in India or Pakistan, it is impolite not to face him directly and look him directly in the eye, but among friends these variables are not so rigidly regulated. There was high agreement that eye contact is more important than shoulder axis. Not standing close to a person or not touching a person in India or Pakistan is not to BE close to a person. To touch a person is a sign of affection, and one Pakistani subject said that the roles for touching are reversed in the U.S. and Pakistan regarding male-female relationships. Too little eye contact in India and Pakistan means that a person is shy, and more than a normal amount means either anger or an attempt to show a person that he has a 'magnetic' personality and that one is attracted to what he is saying. As far as voice loudness is concerned, if an Indian or Pakistani does not know a person too well, it is impolite to speak too loudly. Speaking too loudly also conveys an attempt at dominance.

Latins

The Latin American subjects responded in much the same way as the Arabs. Most said that turning away or not facing directly means a lack of interest, and that shoulder axis is less important than eye contact. Latins generally felt that Americans used more distance in their conversations and that this distance would seem 'cold' in Latin America. One student from Ecuador said that standing in line for tickets in the United States made him nervous because of the space between people. Speaking of waiting to get tickets for a soccer game, the same subject said, "There are no lines in Ecuador." One Latin subject, from El Salvador, mentioned that Latins shake hands with each other and remain where they are to talk, whereas Americans shook hands and stepped back. It is considered unusual not to touch in Latin America, but is seen as a personal preference. The most frequently mentioned difference between Americans and Latins was the amount of eye contact during a conversation. Latins seem to make much more use of their eyes than Americans. Not to look in the eye is considered to be suspicious, dishonest, and conveys a lack of interest among Latins. A subject from Ecuador said that he was appalled to see President Johnson on television at the Pan American conference at Punta del Este in 1967 wearing dark glasses, ostensibly to shield his eyes from the television lights. The Ecuadorean said that he would not be surprised if all the Latin American leaders at the conference felt a little distrustful of Johnson because of the dark glasses. Another subject, from Puerto Rico, said that it was common to arrange people at a table so that everyone could see everyone else. The Latins generally agreed that Americans usually talked at a lower voice level, which is considered suspicious or shy. Some subjects said that when they had conversations with other Latins in the presence of Americans, the Americans frequently thought that the Latins were angry, but this was not the case. Latins, it seems, raise their voices when they get excited about something, or to make a point. Latins also mentioned that Americans were sometimes louder, at a fraternity party for example. One Puerto Rican summed up the Latin attitude toward this type of loudness by eloquently saying, "This is not personal involvement, but just a lot of people screaming." And a Venezuelan said that behaving like a North American in Latin America would be considered distant and snobbish.

Northern Europeans

Interviews with Northern Europeans did not yield nearly as much information as among other groups. This is due to the fact that most Northern Europeans felt that Americans were very similar to them in proxemic behavior. One interesting piece of information which did emerge, however, was the comment that directness of facing and eye contact went hand in hand. These remarks were made by German, Dutch, and Norwegian subjects, and contrast with remarks made by Arabs, Indians-Pakistanis, and Latins. Most Northern Europeans said that they were nervous when approached too closely, and tried to back away. As far as touching is concerned, some subjects of the Northern European group felt that they shook hands more frequently than Americans, and therefore touched more. An English subject said that not to touch other people is "bred into you". An Australian subject mentioned that he could not imagine a situation where one would touch a great deal, as this just is not done in Australia, and did not know what he would do in such a situation. One German subject said that the only situation he could think of in which one man would touch another was when a person made a joke at the expense of a friend and would touch the friend to assure him that it was all in fun. Some Northern European subjects felt that a person should look another in the eye to convey an impression of honesty and sincerity. Raising the voice seems characteristically to convey anger among Northern Europeans. One subject, a Scot, felt that Northern Europeans just were not as expressive as some other groups, notably Southern Europeans. He felt that a standard Scottish joke pointed out the dullness of the Scots: A newspaper in Scotland sponsored a contest wherein the first prize was a week's vacation in Edinburgh, and second prize was two weeks.

Southern Europeans

The Southern Europeans responded with similar ideas as the Arabs and Latins. Being less direct than normal means indifference. More distance means, as one French subject put it, a "lack of harmony". Another Frenchman commented that Americans always backed up when he talked to them. Southern Europeans felt they touch each other more than Americans did, and not to do so would be unfriendly. The Americans are not as expressive with their eyes, and less eye contact would convey a feeling of insincerity to a Southern European. "A good speaker must look into your eyes", a Turkish student said. The Southern Europeans, like the Arabs and Latins, felt that raising the level of the voice means excitement or expression of emotion, not necessarily anger.

PROXEMIC INTERFERENCE AND ALIENATION FROM INTERACTION

It will be recalled that in Chapter I mention was made of personal, or individual, distance in animals. Personal distance was defined by Condor

(1949) and Hediger (1941) as the distance an animal keeps between itself and members of its own species. Humans also keep similar distances, or zones, between themselves and their fellows. Hall (1966: 121) describes these zones as 'bubbles' around a person which are extensions of his personality. The dimensions of these zones, furthermore, varies from culture to culture. Westley and MacLean (1957, in Smith, 1966: 81), in discussing interpersonal interactions, write: "Face-to-face communication involves more sense modalities. It also provides immediate 'feedback' ... In other words, more senses ... can come into play in the person-person act than in any other situation." Hall (1966: 108-120) has further explained that there are various degrees of sensory involvement in face-to-face interactions, i.e., the closer one person is to another during an interaction, the more sensory involvement is present. Proxemic behavior can then be seen as interactions within a particular culture at fairly uniform distances in a given situation. The people of a particular culture can be viewed as carrying around with them 'bubbles' of roughly the same size.

Further, these "bubbles" are carried around by humans largely "outside awareness" (Hall, 1955: 84-85; 1959: 73-74; 1964: 41; 1966: 109), i.e., people are not conscious of the importance of maintaining these distances until violations of these norms occur, most typically in a cross-cultural interaction. Due to proxemic behavior being largely outside awareness, it is difficult for a person to present a proxemic façade to the world. (See Goffman, 1959 for an insightful discussion of the façades people can present to the world.) It is difficult, then, for an individual to control and manipulate his pattern of proxemic behavior.

All of the points made above bring us to the importance of proxemic interference. When two patterns of proxemic behavior meet in an interaction, there is likely to be "interference between [the] two patterns, or a perceived absence of patterning, during an encounter" (Hall, 1963b: 1005). These interferences can lead to discomfort and even illness (Hall, 1963a: 423), but more frequently to misunderstanding. When people from cultures with different proxemic patterns interact with one another, they cannot be relied upon to place the same meaning on the same element of proxemic behavior. They then interpret the proxemic behavior of the person from another culture in terms of the proxemic behavior of their own culture; they become aware of a violation of proxemic norms, but perhaps cannot find the source of the violation. Hall (1963b: 1005) has mentioned that his subjects misinterpreted American listening behavior most frequently, and the previous section on the meaning of proxemic behavior gives other sources of misinterpretation. Subjects from contact countries perceive foreigners from non-contact countries to be shy, un-interested, cold, and impolite. On the other hand, non-contact students described people from contact groups as being pushy, aggressive, ob-noxious, and, again, impolite.

Hall's (1963b: 1005) subjects "reported suffering from alienations in encounters with Americans", as did my own subjects. Goffman (1957, in Smith, 1966: 108-111) has described four types of alienation from interac-tion: external preoccupation, self-consciousness, interaction-conscious-ness, and other-consciousness. All of these forms of alienation from interaction follow proxemic interference, but external preoccupation, self-consciousness, and other-consciousness were more frequently mentioned by subjects than interaction-consciousness. External pre-occupation is described by Goffman (1957, in Smith, 1966: 106) as when "the individual may neglect the prescribed focus of attention and give his main concern to something that is unconnected with what is being talked about at the time and even unconnected with the other persons present...". During an interaction external preoccupation does not actually have to exist for behavior to be interpreted as such. Thus, many contact subjects in the sample mentioned that turning away and less eye contact, which were observed when talking to Americans, gave the impression that Americans were not interested in the conversation. Goffman (1957, in Smith, 1966: 108) explains other-consciousness as occurring when "during interaction, the individual may become distracted by another participant as an object of attention — exactly as in the case of self-consciousness he can become distracted by concern over himself". A person is bewildered by an interaction with another person displaying different proxemic behavior; his attention is focused on the other person. A member of a contact group may wonder why a non-contact American backs up during a conversation, or has such a suspiciously low voice level. The American, conversely, is puzzled by the audacity of a Latin American or an Arab, whom he has just met, who tries to get closer to him and keeps trying to touch him during a conversation. Each interactant focuses his attention on the other, wondering why he does not act in the 'proper' way, which is defined by the situation. During a period of proxemic interference, after other-consciousness has occurred, an individual's attention may switch from the other person to himself. He may become self-conscious. Self-consciousness, according to Goffman (1957, in Smith, 1966: 106) occurs in the following manner: "At the cost of his involvement in the prescribed focus of attention, the individual may focus his attention more than he ought upon himself — himself as someone who is faring well or badly, as

someone calling forth a desirable or undesirable response from others."
When a person perceives an absence of proxemic patterning in his conversational partner, attention is focused on the other person as a source
of the interference. He then, perhaps, focuses his attention on himself as
the source of the trouble, searching for clues in his own behavior which
may have triggered such 'odd' responses in the person he is trying to talk
to. In either case he is paying more attention to the behavior of the interactants and not enough to the topic of conversation. Both other-consciousness and self-consciousness occur at the expense of involvement
with the other person. The Puerto Rican subject, mentioned in the previous
section, provided a good illustration when he said that Americans being
loud at parties did not represent people involved in one another, but just a
lot of noise. Many contact subjects mentioned similar thoughts. They felt
Americans were dull, uninterested, and shy; Americans display a lack of
involvement. Goffman (1957, in Smith, 1966: 110) writes: "... when members of different groups interact with one another, it is quite likely that at
least one of the participants will be distracted from spontaneous involvement in the topic of conversation because of what appears to him to be un-
suitable behavior on the part of the others." It might be added that when
interactants are members of contact and non-contact groups, distraction
is almost inevitable.

In terms of interferences involved, an interesting contrast can be made
between proxemic interference and linguistic interference. A person knows
immediately when linguistic interference is taking place, and knows the
cause. It may be a word he does not understand, or a whole language.
When proxemic interference occurs, a person generally knows SOMETHING
is going wrong, but cannot put his finger on it, at least immediately.

PROXEMIC BEHAVIOR AND THE GENERAL CLASSIFICATION MODEL

Although Hall's (1963b: 1003, 1964: 41, 1966: 1) definitions of proxemics, cited in the Introduction, are broad enough to include proxemic
behavior in both the 'environmental props' and 'self-marker' categories
of Altman and Lett's (1967) general classification model, the research
reported in this dissertation is concerned primarily with proxemic
behavior as a part of the 'self-marker' category. It should be emphasized
here that proxemic behavior on the interpersonal level is only ONE part of
the 'self-marker' category, as other systems of somatic communication
play a role in an interaction. Darwin (1872: 365), for instance, described,

almost a century ago, the importance of facial expression and body position as a communicative device: "The movements of expression in the face and body ... are in themselves of much importance for our welfare." More recently, Ekman's (1964) experiments show that people have the ability to correctly indicate the relationship between photographs of interactants and verbal behavior using the head and body as cues. La Barre (1956) describes different ways in which people of different cultures use their bodies to gesture and display their feelings. Birdwhistell's (1952, 1960, 1966) work demonstrates that kinesics, which he defines as "... the study of body motion as related to the non-verbal aspects of interpersonal communication" (1952: 3), also belongs in the 'self-marker' category of the model. The preceding statements, then, illustrate that proxemics is not the only system of communication present in the 'self-marker' category, but it is the only one which concerns us here.

It should be clear from the section in this chapter on the meanings of proxemic behavior that proxemic behavior COMMUNICATES. In some cultures, for example, raising one's voice indicates excitement or eagerness to make one's point, while in other cultures it may indicate loss of self-control or anger. Gazing intently into the eyes of another person might communicate interest in what the speaker is saying; in another culture it might mean a threat or an attempt to embarrass the other person. In terms of Altman and Lett's (1967) model (Figure 3), when people from the same cultural group interact, things go smoothly; or cues are interpreted and readjustment process takes place or a new situation is defined. When two people from the same cultural group interact, they have a great degree of control over the interaction in that they share bases on which to define the situation. When two people from the same culture begin an interaction they have a common knowledge of how the situation is to be defined from the antecedent factors mentioned in the model. If each of them have 'sized up' the situation properly, i.e., have subjective expectations of the interaction, things will go smoothly until the interaction is broken off. If the interactants do not define the situation in the same way, then, looking only at proxemic behavior, a readjustment is made, or a new situation is defined by using the 'self-marker' category in the model. Suppose that in a particular culture person A and person B enter an interaction. Person A determines his relationship to person B by means of antecedent factors, e.g., B's clothing, his accent, his emotional state, his degree of acquaintance to A, the time of day, the setting all help A to define the situation. And the same things help B to define the situation. If A sums up the antecedent factors and judges B to be of lower status, then he will act accordingly. If B determines from the antecendent factors that A is his superior and acts accordingly, both persons will have defined the situation in the same way and the interaction will probably proceed according to the expectations of both interactants. Suppose, however, that A judges B to be his inferior, but B, by some oversight, fails to recognize A as his superior and fails to act toward A in the way which the culture specifies that someone should act toward a person of higher status. B may violate cultural norms in interacting with A, and A may cue him to readjust his behavior and redefine his relationship with A. If B violates proxemic norms A would 'put him in his place' by using proxemic 'self-markers' as cues to communicate B's inferiority. A may stand closer to B, or farther away; he may raise his voice or lower it; he might look B in the eye or look away, etc., according to cultural pre-scriptions. Or we could imagine a situation in which B could intentionally ignore A's cues in order to show his contempt for A, or to produce conflict, or for any number of reasons. But imagine two well-meaning persons from different cultures, with different proxemic patterns, entering an interaction. Neither has the culturally specific information with which to define the situation in terms of the other's expectations. Both persons might define the situation as one which calls for a personal interaction in a public place, but the distance, directness, amount of touching and eye contact, and voice level specified by each culturally-defined system of proxemic behavior might be different. This would leave both parties in the interaction constantly readjusting their behavior to fit expectations at the cost of involvement with the other person. Altman and Lett (1967: 17) summarize this dilemma:

An inconsistency in A's and B's personal definition of the situation is important as a potential initial determinant of interpersonal conflict and stress. To the extent that there is a discrepancy in their expectations, there will be a reverbera-tion throughout the remainder of the model ... Each person would begin ex-periencing unanticipated behaviors on the other's part, which eventually could be the basis for an incompatible relationship.

Thus, there lurks hidden in intercultural communications the danger of misinterpretation of proxemic patterns at the cost of involvement, and without involvement an interaction loses the transactional qualities which must be present in order for people to understand each other.

VI

SUMMARY AND CONCLUSIONS

SUMMARY

The research reported in this dissertation is concerned with proxemic behavior on the interpersonal level; how man structures microspace in face-to-face encounters with other persons and "how he relates physically to other persons with whom he is interacting, and what is communicated by these physical relationships" (Watson and Graves, 1966: 971).

The review of the literature pointed out the importance of the structuring of space in animals. It is, indeed, often a life or death matter. Increasing knowledge of man's structuring of space suggests that it is as vital to humans as it is to other animals — perhaps as basic a need as food or sex (Hall, 1963a: 422). Despite the importance of the structuring of space by humans, very little is known about it. This research is an attempt to gain insight into one level of proxemic behavior, the structuring of space on the interpersonal level.

The ways in which humans perceive and structure microspace is a function of all of his senses; how humans determine whether another person is near or far is a "synthesis of many sensory inputs: visual, auditory, kinesthetic, olfactory, and thermal" (Hall, 1966: 172). Proxemic behavior, for the purposes of this research, is operationally defined along five dimensions: axis (directness of facing), kinesthetic factors (closeness), touching, visual factors (eye contact), and voice loudness.

As very little is known about proxemic behavior the purposes of this research were many: to observe and quantify a large cross-cultural range of proxemic behavior; to test the pertinence of the operationally defined categories used in the observations; to gain insight into the learning and meaning of proxemic behavior; to test the role of various factors in changing proxemic behavior; and, finally, to gain an understanding of how the system of proxemic behavior operates.

To accomplish these ends, a sample of 110 foreign students and 16

American students studying at the University of Colorado was used. The proxemic behavior of subjects from the same country and interacting in pairs in a controlled laboratory setting was observed and recorded. Further, foreign students completed a questionnaire giving basic demographic and experiential information. Foreign students were also interviewed in a semi-structured, open-ended fashion.

CONCLUSIONS

Interesting differences in proxemic behavior of subjects from different parts of the world were revealed from the observations. Quantification of proxemic behavior suggested that the sample was divided into two groups, a 'contact' type and a 'non-contact' type, as has been suggested by Hall (1963b: 1023, 1964: 44-45). A contact group is composed of members who face one another more directly, interact closer to one another, touch one another more, look one another in the eye more, and speak in a louder voice than do members of the non-contact group. The contact group was composed of Arabs, Latin Americans, and Southern Europeans, while Asians, Indians and Pakistanis, and Northern Europeans made up the non-contact group.

In an attempt to get at how proxemic behavior is learned and transmitted, subjects were asked about rules of proxemic behavior. Very few of these rules emerged, and subjects generally agreed that proxemic behavior is learned by imitation.

Many insights were gained into the meanings attached to proxemic norms, and evidence supported the idea that people from different cultures cannot be relied upon to attach the same meaning to the same elements of proxemic behavior. Thus, when people from cultures employing different patterns of proxemic behavior interact, interference is likely to occur with consequent alienation from interaction. Discussions with subjects concerning the meaning of proxemic behavior also demonstrated that the categories of proxemics used in observations were valid and pertinent, and no new categories were uncovered.

Subjects' impressions of American proxemic behavior generally conformed to empirical data, and placed limitations on the stereotype of the loud, 'pushy' American.

Very little influence of Western, urban-industrial culture on proxemic behavior was uncovered. Proxemic behavior seems to remain stable in the presence of urban experience and other sources of contact with Western culture, with the exception of touching within contact groups.

Many interesting relationships among proxemic variables were uncovered in the analysis of the data. The construct of 'contact' and 'non-contact' was supported on a high level of abstraction, but the data seem to suggest that sub-systems may be operable within a general proxemic system. Thus, 'contact' and 'non-contact' might better be defined by closeness and touching, while axis and eye contact might be used to define a 'direct-indirect' syndrome. Voice loudness seemed to be the least diagnostic variable, although this might have been the result of an artificial environment.

SUGGESTIONS FOR FURTHER RESEARCH

Suggestions for further research are traditionally headed by justifications for such research. In the case of research in proxemic behavior such justifications are easy to come by. Hall (1966: 177) provides an eloquent one:

Anthropologists and psychologists must discover how to compute peoples' involvement ratios in a reasonably simple way ... In order to plan intelligently we must have quantitative measures of such involvement. Once we know how to compute involvement ratios, questions for which we will need answers are: What is maximum, minimum, and ideal density for rural, urban, and transition groups? What is the maximum viable size of the different groups living under urban conditions before normal social controls begin to break down? ... How can space be used therapeutically to help relieve social tensions and cure social ills?

There are enough suggestions in the above passage to keep researchers busy for years to come. Proxemic behavior on the interpersonal level can also provide clues to the annoying and seemingly mysterious interferences which frequently occur in cross-cultural communication. Briefly, proxemic behavior is an important and inadequately understood aspect of human behavior, about which more needs to be known. As more is known about the structuring of space in humans, there will hopefully be no need to repeat Sommer's (1959: 247) statement: "Surprisingly little is known about the way people use space... An almost unexplored area is microecology or the way that people in pairs or small groups arrange themselves."

One of the primary prerequisites to the understanding of proxemic behavior is the use of larger samples. The data reported upon in this research suggest that many surprising interrelationships may exist between proxemic variables, but until a single, culturally specific system of proxemic behavior is understood, our knowledge of these possible relationships is limited. If a large sample of, say, Arab proxemic behavior was observed in a laboratory setting and then in a naturalistic environment, a better understanding of Arab proxemic patterns would be the result. Emphasis should be on UNOBTRUSIVE OBSERVATION. (See Webb *et al.*, 1966 for a full discussion of unobtrusive measures.)

Culturally specific proxemic research could also yield insights illuminating the linkage of proxemic behavior with status and role. In our own North American non-contact culture, for instance, what attitudes prevail toward occupations whose practitioners, due to the nature of their jobs, violate proxemic norms? Several occupations come immediately to mind: physicians, dentists, masseurs, and athletes. North American proxemic norms dictate that men do not ordinarily touch other men, yet blatant violations of these norms occur constantly at football, basketball, and baseball games in the form of players patting the posteriors of other players, and in front of thousands of people.

Linkage of proxemic behavior to other elements of culture also needs to be explored. What is the relationship of proxemic norms to social and political organization, child rearing, or religion? Not only do we need to know how an Arab, for example, learns the proxemic norms of his culture, but also how did Arabs in general come to behave proxemically the way they do.

This research has lent support to Hall's (1963b: 1003) notion that proxemic behavior is largely outside of a person's awareness, and thus very little pertinent information of a person's own proxemic system can be uncovered by direct questioning. Controlled observation appears to be a strategy with greater potential.

A more specific suggestion for further research concerns African proxemic behavior. Although the African sample was eliminated from most of the analysis of the data due to its small size, the African subjects suggested that there was a dichotomy of proxemic behavior between East and West Africa. Eventually the proxemic behavior of entire culture areas could be mapped.

Other research possibilities lie within the context of Altman and Lett's (1967) general classification model, mentioned in the preceding chapter. In the present research the situation was controlled as much as possible, although small samples have limited the ability to control one factor while testing for another. The room in which subjects were observed was kept at a steady temperature level, a steady light level, and a steady noise level. Each pair of subjects was from the same country and spoke the same native language. Each subject of a pair was acquainted with the other member of the pair, except in one instance. Work needs to be done manipulating these various factors in order to see what effect they have on proxemic behavior. What happens when the temperature of the setting is raised or lowered? What is the result of a lower light level or a higher noise level? Do people from the same country behave proxemically the same toward each other if they are not acquainted as when they are best friends? Does female-female or male-female proxemic behavior differ from male-male? Briefly, what situational variables are influential in proxemic behavior? Hall (1966: 171) puts it: "The study of culture in the proxemic sense is therefore the study of people's use of their sensory apparatus in different emotional states during different activities, in different relationships, and in different settings and contexts."

Sorokin (1943: 122) wrote that "the adequate definition of socio-cultural space and of its properties is a task that exceeds the limited capacity of a single investigator. It is a task for the collective work of probably several generations of social scientists...". More investigators from the social sciences are turning their attention to the use of the environment in interpersonal interactions, which brightens Sorokin's pessimistic statement.

APPENDIX A

PROXEMICS RESEARCH QUESTIONNAIRE

MW 42666

1. Name
2. Age (years to nearest birthday)
3. Nationality
4. Native Language
5. Other Languages   speak   understand   read
   a.
   b.
   c.
   d.
6. Urban Experience
   How many years have you lived in urban areas of about 50,000 population or more?
7. Foreign Experience
   a. How many months have you spent outside your native country?
      (1) Traveling for pleasure?   months
      (2) Studying abroad?   months
      (3) Business activities?   months
   b. How many months of this time were spent in Europe?
                  months
   c. How many months have you spent in the United States?
                  months
8. How well are you acquainted with the person who is here with you today? (Circle one)

casual acquaintance	know slightly	know fairly well	good friend	best friend

APPENDIX B

MW 42666

1. When you first came to the U.S., did you notice anything different about the way Americans behaved when talking to each other?
2. When you talked to Americans, in what ways did they act that were different from the ways people act in your country?
3. Did any of the things Americans did bother you?
4. In your country, if someone acts this way, what would it mean?
5. How would you refer to or behave toward a person who acted this way in your country? (Repeat for each behavior mentioned)
6. To make sure we've covered everything, here are some points other students have raised. How about the way Americans:
   a. Sit or stand when talking to each other?
   b. Face you?
   c. Distance from you?
   d. Touching while talking?
   e. Look at you?
   f. Loudness of voice?
7. a. Does anything about the way Americans (supply categories above) bother you?
   b. Is anything about this different from the way people (supply category) in your country?
8. a. In your country, do you have any rules about the way people should (supply category) when talking to each other?
   b. How are those rules learned?
9. a. Are there differences in (supply category) within your own country?
   b. How about the way other people besides Americans (supply category)?

BIBLIOGRAPHY

Allee, W. C.
1934 "Recent studies in mass physiology", *Biological Reviews* 9:1-48.
1958 *The social life of animals* (Boston, Beacon).
Altman, I. and W. W. Haythorn
1967 "The ecology of isolated groups", *Behavioral Science* 12:169-182.
Altman, I. and E. Lett
1967 "The ecology of interpersonal relationships: a classification system and conceptual model", paper presented at the conference on social-psychological factors in stress (University of Illinois, April 10-12, 1967).
Altmann, Stuart A.
1962 "Social behavior of anthropoid primates: analysis of recent concepts", *Roots of behavior*, E. L. Bliss, ed. (N.Y., Harper). 277-285.
Ardrey, R.
1966 *The territorial imperative* (N.Y., Atheneum).
Argyle, M. and J. Dean
1965 "Eye-contact, distance, and affiliation", *Sociometry* 28:289-304.
Aries, Philippe
1962 *Centuries of childhood* (N.Y., Knopf).
Associated Press
1967a "LBJ gives report on summit", *The Denver Post* (Saturday, June 24, 1967).
1967b "Go-going craze-y way to go", *The Denver Post* (Thursday, July 6, 1967).
Bandura, A.
1962 "Social learning through imitation", *Nebraska symposium on motivation* (Lincoln, Nebraska) 211-269.
Barker, R. G. and L. S. Barker
1961 "Behavior units for the comparative study of cultures", *Studying personality cross-culturally*, B. Kaplan, ed. (N.Y., Row Peterson).
Bass, B. M. and S. Klubeck
1952 "Effects of seating arrangement on leaderless group discussions", *Jour. of Abnormal and Social Psychology* 47:724-727.
Belo, Jane
1956 "The Balinese temper", *Personal character and cultural milieu*, D. G. Haring, ed, (Syracuse, N.Y., Syracuse University Press), 157-180.
Best, J. B. and I. Rubinstein
1962 "Environmental familiarity and feeding in the Planarian", *Science* 135:916-918.
Birdwhistell, R. L.
1952 *Introduction to kinesics* (Washington, D.C., Foreign Service Institute, U.S. Department of State).

1960 "Kinesics and communication", *Explorations in communication*, E. Carpenter and M. McLuhan, eds. (Boston, Beacon).
1966 "Some relations between American kinesics and spoken American English", *Communication and culture*, A. G. Smith, ed. (N.Y., Holt, Rinehart, and Winston), 182-189.

Blalock, H. M.
1960 *Social statistics* (N.Y., McGraw-Hill).

Block, H. A. and A. Niederhoffer
1958 *The Gang* (N.Y., Philosophical Library).

Bogardus, E. S.
1933 "A social distance scale", *Sociology and Social Research* 17:265—271.
1959 *Social distance* (Yellow Springs, Ohio, Antioch Press).

Buettner-Janusch, John
1966 *Origins of man* (New York, John Wiley and Sons).

Burt, W. H.
1943 "Territoriality and home range concept as applied to mammals", *Jour. of Mammalogy* 24:346-352.
1949 "Territoriality", *Jour. of Mammalogy* 30:25-27.

Calhoun, J. B.
1952 "The social aspects of population dynamics", *Jour. of Mammalogy* 33:139-159.
1956 "A comparative study of the social behavior of two inbred strains of house mice", *Ecological Monographs* 26:81-103.
1962a "A behavioral sink" *Roots of behavior*, Eugene L. Bliss, ed. (N.Y., Harper and Bros). 295-315.
1962b "Population density and social pathology", *Scientific American* 206 (Feb.): 139-148.

Carpenter, C. R.
1934 "A field study of the behavior and social relations of howling monkeys (Alouatta palliata)", *Comparative Psychology Monographs* 10:1-168.
1935 "Behavior of red spider monkeys in Panama", *Jour. of Mammalogy* 16:171-180.
1940 "A field study in Siam of the behavior and social relations of the gibbon (Hylobates lar)", *Comparative Psychology Monographs* 16:1-212.
1958 "Territoriality: A review of concepts and problems", *Behavior and evolution*, A. Roe and G. G. Simpson, eds. (New Haven, Yale University Press), 224-250.

Carpenter, E. and M. McLuhan
1960 "Acoustic space", *Explorations in communication* (Boston, Beacon), 65-70.

Castiglione, Baldesar
1959 *The book of the courtier*, translated by C. S. Singleton (Garden City, N.Y., Anchor).

Chance, M. R. A.
1962 "An interpretation of some agonistic postures", *Symposia of the Zoological Society of London* 8:71-89.

Christian, J. J., V. Flyger, and D. E. Davis
1960 "Factors in mass mortality of a herd of sika deer (Cervus nippon)", *Chesapeake Science* 1:79-95.

Clark, D.
1962 "Experimental studies of the behavior of an aggressive predatory mouse, Onychomys leucogaster", *Roots of behavior*, E. L. Bliss, ed., 179-186.

Condor, P. J.
1949 "Individual distance", *Ibis* 91:649-655.

Darwin, C.
1872   *The expression of the emotions in man and animals* (London, Murry).
Davis, D. E.
1962   "An inquiry into the phylogeny of gangs", *Roots of behavior*, E. L. Bliss, ed., 316-320.
Dethier, V. G. and E. Stellar
1961   *Animal behavior* (Englewood Cliffs, N.J., Prentice Hall).
Eibl-Eibesfeldt, Irenaus
1961   "The fighting behaviour of animals", *Scientific American* 205 (Dec.):112-122.
Ekman, Paul
1964   "Body position, facial expression, and verbal behavior during interviews", *Jour. of Abnormal and Social Psychology* 68:295-301.
Errington, P.
1938   "The great horned owl as an indication of vulnerability in the prey populations", *Jour. of Wildlife Management* 2:190-205.
1956   "Factors limiting higher vertebrate populations", *Science* 124:304-307.
Esser, A. H., S. Amparo, R. N. Chamberlain, E. D. Chapple and N. S. Kline
1964   "Territoriality of patients on a research ward", *Recent Advances in Biological Psychiatry* 7:37-44.
Felipe, Nancy
1966   "Interpersonal distance and small group interaction", *Cornell Jour. of Social Relations* 1:59-64.
Ferguson, G. A.
1959   *Statistical analysis in psychology and education* (N.Y., McGraw-Hill).
Feshbach, S. and N. Feshbach
1963   "Influence of the stimulus object upon the complementary and supplementary projection of fear", *Jour. of Abnormal and Social Psychology* 66:498-502.
Frank, Lawrence K.
1957   "Tactile communication", *Genetic Psychology Monographs* 56:209-255. *In Communication and Culture*, A. G. Smith, ed. (N.Y., Holt, Rinehart and Winston), 1966:199-209.
1960   "Tactile communication", *Explorations in communication*, E. Carpenter and M. McLuhan, eds. (Boston, Beacon), 4-11.
Gibson, J. J.
1950   *The perception of the visual world* (Boston, Houghton Mifflin).
Giedion, S.
1960   "Space conception in prehistoric art", *Explorations in communication*, E. Carpenter and M. McLuhan, eds. (Boston, Beacon), 71-89.
Goffman, E.
1957   "Alienation from interaction", *Human Relations* 10:47-60. *In Communication and culture*, A. G. Smith, ed. (N.Y., Holt, Rinehart, and Winston), 103-118.
1959   *The presentation of self in everyday life* (Garden City, N.Y., Anchor).
Goode, W. J. and P. K. Hatt
1952   *Methods in social research* (N.Y., McGraw-Hill).
Hall, E. T.
1955   "The anthropology of manners", *Scientific American* 162 (April):85-90.
1959   *The silent language* (Greenwich, Conn., Fawcett).
1960   "The silent language in overseas business", *Harvard Business Review* 38 (May-June):87-96.
1961   "The language of space", *Jour. of the American Institute of Architects* 35 (Feb.):71-74.
1963a "Proxemics — the study of man's spatial relations", *Man's image in medicine and anthropology*, I. Galdston ed. (N.Y., International Universities Press), 422-445.

1963b "A system for the notation of proxemic behavior", *American Anthropologist* 65:1003-1026.

1964 "Silent assumptions in social communication", *Disorders of Communication* 42:41-55.

1966 *The hidden dimension* (New York, Doubleday).

1967 Personal communication.

Hall, E. T. and W. F. Whyte

1960 "Intercultural communication: a guide to men of action", *Human Organization* 19:5567-576.

Hare, A. P. and R. F. Bales

1963 "Seating position and small group interaction", *Sociometry* 26:480-486.

Hearn, G.

1957 "Leadership and the spatial factor in small groups" *Jour. of Abnormal and social Psychology* 54:269-272.

Hediger, H.

1941 *Biologische Gesetzmässigkeiten im Verhalten von Wirbeltieren* (Bern, Mitteilung Naturwissenschaft Gesellschaft Bern).

1950 *Wild animals in captivity* (London, Butterworths).

1955 *Studies of the psychology and behavior of captive animals in zoos and circuses* (London, Butterworths),

1961 "The evolution of territorial behavior", *Social life of early man* S. L. Washburn, ed. (N.Y., *Viking Fund Publications in Anthropology* 31).

Hewes, G. W.

1955 "World distribution of certain postural habits", *American Anthropologist* 57:231-234.

Hogg, J.

1854 "Observations on the development and growth of the water snail (Lymnaeus stagnaus)", *Quarterly Jour. of Microscopical Science* 2:91-103.

Horowitz, M. J.

1963 "Graphic communication: a study of interaction painting with schizophrenics", *American Jour. of Psychotherapy* 17:230-239.

Howard, H. E.

1920 *Territory in bird life* (London, Murray).

Howells, L. T. and S. W. Becker

1962 "Seating arrangement and leadership emergence", *Jour. of Abnormal and Social Psychology* 64:148-150.

Hutt, C. and C. Ounsted

1966 "The biological significance of gaze aversion with particular reference to the syndrome of infantile autism", *Behavioral Science* 11:346-356.

Jolly, Alison

1966 *Lemur behavior* (Chicago, University of Chicago Press).

Joos, Martin

1962 *The five clocks* (N.Y., Harcourt, Brace, and World).

Kelela, O.

1954 "Range possession as a factor of population ecology in birds and mammals", *Vanamo* 16:1-48.

Kates, R. W. and J. F. Wohlwill

1966 "Man's response to the physical environment: Introduction", *Jour. of Social Issues* 22:15-21.

Kolaja, Jiri

1954 "A note on the spatial and social pattern of a small discussion group", *Jour. of Educational Sociology* 27:222-224.

Kortland, A.
1962 "Chimpanzees in the wild", *Scientific American* 206 (May):128-138.
Kuethe, J. L.
1962a "Social schemas", *Jour. of Abnormal and Social Psychology* 64:31-38.
1962b "Social schemas and the reconstruction of social object displays from memory", *Jour. of Abnormal and Social Psychology* 65:71-74.
Kuethe, J. L. and H. Weingartner
1964 "Male-female schemata of homosexual and non-homosexual penitentiary inmates", *Jour. of Personality* 32:23-31.
LaBarre, W.
1954 *The human animal* (Chicago, University of Chicago Press).
1956 "The cultural basis of emotions and gestures", *Personal character and cultural milieu*, D. G. Haring, ed. (Syracuse, N.Y., Syracuse University Press), 547-563.
Leavitt, H. J.
1951 "Some effects of certain communication patterns on group performance", *Jour. of Abnormal and Social Psychology* 46:38-50.
Life Magazine
1966 "Tools to reach beyond the boundaries of man's vision" 61 (Dec. 23):105-120.
Little, K. B.
1965 "Personal space", *Jour. of Experimental Social Pyschology* 1:237-247.
Lorenz, K.
1966 *On aggression* (N.Y., Harcourt, Brace, and World).
Lowie, R. H.
1938 *The history of ethnological theory* (N.Y., Holt, Rinehart, and Winston).
Lynch, K.
1960 *The image of the city* (Cambridge, MIT Press).
Mair, L.
1962 *Primitive government* (N.Y., Penguin).
McLuhan, M.
1964 *Understanding media* (N.Y., McGraw-Hill).
Michelmore, S.
1964 *Sexual reproduction* (N.Y., Anchor).
Montagu, M. F. A. and C. L. Brace
1965 *Man's evolution: an introduction to physical anthropology* (N.Y., MacMillan).
Mowat, F.
1963 *Never cry wolf* (Boston, Little, Brown).
Murphy, R. F.
1964 "Social distance and the veil", *American Anthropologist* 66:1257-1274.
Osmond, H.
1957 "Function as the basis of psychiatric ward design", *Mental Hospitals* (April): 23-29.
1959 "The history and social development of mental hospitals", *Psychiatirc architecture*, C. Goshen, ed. (Washington, D.C., American Psychiatric Association), 7-9.
Ovid
1957 *The art of love*, translated by Rolf Humphries (Bloomington, Indiana, University of Indiana Press).
Parkes, A. S. and H. M. Bruce
1961 "Olfaction stimuli in mammalian reproduction", *Science* 134:1049-1054.
Pike, K. L.
1966 "Etic and emic standpoints for the description of behavior", *Communication and culture*, A. G. Smith, ed. (N.Y., Holt, Rinehart, and Winston).

Playboy Magazine
　1967　"Playboy after hours" 14(July):21-23.
Russell, W. M. S.
　1966　"Aggression: new light from animals", *New Society* 7:12-14.
Schaller, G. B.
　1965　*The year of the gorilla* (N.Y., Ballantine).
Scott, J. P.
　1962　"Hostility and aggression in animals", *Roots of behavior*, E. L. Bliss, ed., 167-178.
Segall, M. H., D. T. Campbell, and M. J. Herskovits
　1966　*The influence of culture on visual perception* (Indianapolis, Bobbs-Merrill).
Selye, H.
　1956　*The stress of life* (N.Y., McGraw-Hill).
Service, E. R.
　1962　*Primitive social organization* (N.Y., Random House).
Shoemaker, H.
　1939　"Social hierarchy in flocks of the canary", *The Auk* 56:381-406.
Sommer, R.
　1959　"Studies in personal space", *Sociometry* 22:247-260.
　1961　"Leadership and group geography", *Sociometry* 24:99-110.
　1962　"The distance for comfortable conversation: a further study", *Sociometry* 25:111-116.
　1966　"The ecology of privacy", *The Library Quarterly* 36:234-248.
Sorokin, P.
　1943　*Sociocultural causality: Time and space, a study of referential principles of sociology and social science* (Durham, N.C., Duke University Press).
Steinzor, B.
　1950　"The spatial factor in face-to-face discussion groups", *Jour. of Abnormal and Social Psychology* 45:552-555.
Tinbergen, N.
　1951　*The study of instinct* (Oxford, Clarendon Press).
　1952　"The curious behavior of the stickleback", *Scientific American* 187(6):22-26.
Tyrwhitt, J.
　1960　"The moving eye", *Explorations in communication*, E. Carpenter and M. McLuhan, eds. (Boston, Beacon).
Washburn, S. L. and V. Avis
　1958　"Evolution of human behavior", In A. Roe and G. G. Simpson, eds., 421-436.
Washburn, S. L. and I. DeVore
　1961a　"Social behavior of baboons and early man", *Social life of early man*, S. L. Washburn, ed. (Chicago, Aldine), 91-105.
　1961b　"The social life of baboons", *Scientific American* 204 (June):62-71.
Watson, O. M.
　1966　*An atlas of Navaho space*. Unpublished ms.
Watson, O. M. and T. D. Graves
　1966　"Quantitative research in proxemic behavior", *American Anthropologist* 68:971-985.
Webb, E. J., D. T. Campbell, R. D. Schwartz, and L. Sechrest
　1966　*Unobtrusive measures: Nonreactive research in the social sciences* (Chicago, Rand McNally).
Westley, B. H. and M. S. MacLean
　1957　"A conceptual model for communications research", *Journalism Quarterly* 34:31-38. In *Communication and culture*, A. G. Smith, ed. (N.Y., Holt, Rinehart, and Winston), 80-87.

Whorf, B. L.
   1956   "Some verbal categories of Hopi", *In Language, thought and reality*, J. B.
          Carroll, ed. (Cambridge, Mass., MIT Press), 112-124.
Winick, C. and H. Holt
   1961   "Seating positions as non-verbal communication in group analysis", *Psychiatry*
          24:171-182.
Wynne-Edwards, V. C.
   1965   "Self regulatory systems in populations of animals", *Science* 147:1543-1548.

APPROACHES TO SEMIOTICS

edited by

THOMAS A. SEBEOK

assisted by

JULIA KRISTEVA   JOSETTE REY-DEBOVE

Prices are subject to change
Titles without prices are in preparation

MOUTON · PUBLISHERS · THE HAGUE